Making Literacy Real

Theories and Practices for Learning and Teaching

JOANNE LARSON AND JACKIE MARSH

SAGE Publications
London • Thousand Oaks • New Delhi

SAGE Publications Ltd
1 Oliver's Yard
55 City Road
London EC1Y 1SP

SAGE Publications Inc
2455 Teller Road
Thousand Oaks, California 91320

SAGE Publications India Pvt Ltd
B-42, Panchsheel Enclave
Post Box 4109
New Delhi 110 017

British Library Cataloguing in Publication data

A catalogue record for this book is available from the British
Library

ISBN 1-4129-0330-0
ISBN 1-4129-0331-9 (pbk)

Library of Congress Control Number: 2005929233

Typeset by Pantek Arts Ltd, Maidstone, Kent
Printed on paper from sustainable resources
Printed in Great Britain by Athenaeum Press, Gateshead,
Tyne & Wear

To Morris, Anna, Eric, and Marcus

Also to Keith Gallagher, for his inspirational approach to literacy teaching

Contents

Notes on Contributors

Barbara Comber is a key researcher in the Centre for Studies in Literacy, Policy and Learning Cultures and Professor of Education at the University of South Australia. Her research interests include pedagogy, class, classroom discourse, literacy, teachers' work, social justice, critical literacies, and school-based collaborative research. She has conducted a number of in-depth and longitudinal studies of literacy teaching and learning primarily in low socioeconomic status (SES) communities. She is particularly committed to working with teacher-researcher communities. She has recently co-edited three books: *Turn-around Pedagogies: Literacy Interventions for At-risk Students* (Comber and Kamler, 2005) *Look Again: Longitudinal Studies of Children's Literacy Learning* (Comber and Barnett, 2003) and *Negotiating Critical Literacies in Classrooms* (Comber and Simpson, 2001).

Lynn Gatto has taught all grades at the elementary level in the Rochester City School District for over 30 years. She has received numerous local and national awards, including a 2001 Toyota Tapestry Award and the Presidential Award for Excellence in Science and Mathematics Teaching in 1997. Most recently, she was named the 2004 New York State Teacher of the Year. She is a national presenter for educational and research conferences and has published in teacher journals and in literacy research books (Gatto, 2001). She recently completed writing elementary science curriculum modules for a national publishing company. Lynn is a doctoral student in the University of Rochester's Warner Graduate School of Education and Human Development.

Michele Knobel is an Associate Professor of Education at Montclair State University (USA), where she co-ordinates the graduate and undergraduate literacy programs, and an Adjunct Professor of Education at Central Queensland University, Australia. Her research at present focuses on the relationship between new literacies, social practices and digital technologies. Michele's most recent book is *A Handbook for Teacher Research* (with Colin Lankshear). She is currently working on a new literacies primer, *Technoliteracies* (with Colin Lankshear and Angela Thomas), as well as co-editing *The Handbook of Research on New Literacies* (with Donald Leu, Julie Coiro and Colin Lankshear).

Colin Lankshear is a freelance educational researcher and writer based in Mexico where he is a permanent resident. He is currently a half-time Professor of Literacy and New Technologies at James Cook University in Cairns, Australia, an Adjunct Professor of Education at Central Queensland University, Australia, and teaches short courses in Mexico, Canada and the USA. His current research and publishing focus mainly on literacy and other social practices involving new technologies. He is a member of research teams on projects funded by the Australian Research Council and the Australian government, investigating factors associated with low female participation rates in information and communication technology (ICT) professional occupations and 'Success for Boys', respectively. Recent books include *New Literacies: Changing Knowledge and Classroom Learning* (with Michele Knobel), and *Cyber Spaces/Social Spaces: Culture Clash in Computerized Classrooms* (with Ivor Goodson et al.), and he is joint editor of a forthcoming work, *The Handbook of Research on New Literacies*.

Joanne Larson is Associate Professor and Chair of the Teaching and Curriculum program at the University of Rochester's Warner Graduate School of Education and Human Development. She received her PhD at the University of California, Los Angeles in 1995. Drawing on New Literacy Studies, her research focuses on literacy as a social practice and examines the ways in which classroom language and literacy practices mediate access to participation in literacy events in primary classrooms. Her teaching includes courses on curriculum theory, diversity, qualitative research methods, and literacy learning. She has authored articles in *Research in the Teaching of English, Journal of Early Childhood Literacy, Language Arts, Linguistics and Education, Discourse and Society* and *Written Communication;* co-authored articles in *Harvard Educational Review, Urban Education* and the *International Journal of Educational Reform* and has chapters in several books. She is editor of *Literacy as Snake Oil: Beyond the Quick Fix* and co-editor of the *Handbook of Early Childhood Literacy* with Nigel Hall and Jackie Marsh, published by Sage. She has branched out of typical publication venues with the production of a documentary film on the consequences of the No Child Left Behind legislation on teaching and learning in urban classrooms. She has also co-produced a professional development film on teaching literacy in the current reductionist pedagogical context.

Maryrita Maier has been a first grade teacher for her entire career. In fact, until 2002, she had taught first grade in the same school for over 25 years, long enough to be teaching children of children she taught when they were first graders. Maryrita is currently pursuing her doctoral degree with Larson.

Hilary Malden is a teacher at Meersbrook Bank Primary School in Sheffield. Hilary qualified as a teacher in 1979 and taught at several different primary schools before joining Meersbrook Bank. She presented her work on digital literacies at the United Kingdom Literacy Association (UKLA) 2004 conference in Manchester.

Jackie Marsh is a Reader in Education at the University of Sheffield, UK, where she teaches the MA Literacy and Language in Education and MA Early Childhood Education. She recently edited, along with Nigel Hall and Joanne Larson, the *Handbook of Early Childhood Literacy* (Sage, 2003) and is an editor of the *Journal of Early Childhood Literacy*. Jackie is involved in research which examines the role and nature of popular culture and media in early childhood literacy, both in- and out-of-school contexts. She co-directed, with Elaine Millard, the ESRC Research Seminar Series 'Children's Literacy and Popular Culture' (2002–04). Publications in this field include the edited *Popular Culture, Media and Digital Literacy in Early Childhood* (RoutledgeFalmer, 2005) and the co-authored (with Elaine Millard) *Literacy and Popular Culture: Using Children's Culture in the Classroom* (Sage/Paul Chapman, 2000). Jackie is currently President of UKLA.

Barbara Rogoff received her PhD in 1977 from Harvard. She is currently University of California (UC) Santa Cruz Foundation Professor of Psychology and holds the University of California Presidential Chair. She is a Fellow of the American Psychological Society, the American Anthropological Association, and the American Psychological Association. Barbara Rogoff has been a Fellow of the Center for Advanced Study in the Behavioral Sciences, a Kellogg Fellow, a Spencer Fellow, and an Osher Fellow of the Exploratorium. She has served as Editor of *Human Development* and of the *Newsletter of the Society for Research in Child Development*, Study Section member for the National Institute of Child Health and Human Development, and a committee member on the Science of Learning for the National Academy of Science. She was selected to give the 2004 UC Santa

Cruz Faculty Research Lecture. Her book *Apprenticeship in Thinking* (1990) received the Scribner Award from the American Educational Research Association. Recent books include: *Learning Together: Children and Adults in a School Community* (2001), with C. Goodman-Turkanis and L. Bartlett, and *The Cultural Nature of Human Development* (2003).

Brian Street is Professor of Language in Education at King's College London and Visiting Professor of Education in the Graduate School of Education, University of Pennsylvania. He undertook anthropological fieldwork on literacy in Iran during the 1970s, taught social and cultural anthropology for over 20 years at the University of Sussex before taking up the Chair of Language in Education at King's. He has written and lectured extensively on literacy practices from both a theoretical and an applied perspective. In addition to writing, editing and collaborating on ten books, he has published over 60 scholarly articles and given numerous keynote addresses at major international conferences. He has a longstanding commitment to linking ethnographic-style research on the cultural dimension of language and literacy with contemporary practice in education and in development. Books include *Literacy in Theory and Practice* (Cambridge University Press, 1985), edited *Cross-Cultural Approaches to Literacy* (Cambridge University Press, 1993), *Social Literacies* (1995), *Literacy and Development: Ethnographic Perspectives* (ed., Routledge, 2000) and *Literacy across Educational Contexts* (Caslon Press, 2005). He is also currently involved in research projects on academic literacies (co-ed., *Student Writing in the University: Cultural and Epistemological Issues*, Benjamins, 2000) and on home/school literacy and numeracy practices (forthcoming, co-author *Numeracy Practices at Home and at School*, Kluwer).

Vivian Vasquez is an Assistant Professor in the School of Education at American University in Washington, DC, where she teaches undergraduate and graduate literacy courses. Previous to this she taught pre-school and primary school in Canada. Her research is focused on Critical Literacy, Early Literacy, Inquiry and Social Justice. Her latest publications include two books, *Negotiating Critical Literacies with Young Children*, published by Lawrence Erlbaum (2004), and *Getting Beyond I Like the Book-Creating Spaces for Critical Literacy in K-6 Settings*, published by the International Reading Association (2003). Other publications include book chapters and articles published in *Language Arts, Phi Delta Kappa, UKLA Reading, Journal of Adolescent and Adult Literacy, Reading Teacher* and *Reading Today*. Vivian has held appointive and elective offices in scholarly organizations including the National Council of Teachers of English, the American Educational Research Association, the International Reading Association and the Whole Language Umbrella.

Acknowledgments

We are grateful to Marianne Lagrange at Paul Chapman/Sage for her confidence in our ability to put together a theoretical work that teachers and researchers, both novice and expert, can use in their practice. We both honor the work of the teachers/teacher-researchers described in this book and shall always be grateful for their help in telling the stories of their classrooms. We also appreciate the generosity of Guy Merchant and Vivian Vasquez in sharing their insightful research and writing based on the classrooms described. We thank Barbara Comber, Michele Knobel, Colin Lankshear, Barbara Rogoff and Brian Street for their intellectual leadership and for the time they gave to answer our questions.

We both have a number of individuals to thank. Larson and Marsh thank their colleagues and students for the scholarly inspiration behind their research and practice. It makes all the difference in the world to have a positive work context. Finally, Larson is grateful for the love and support of her husband, Morris Smith, and her three children, Anna, Eric, and Marcus, and Marsh for the unremitting patience of her partner, Julie Hooper. Without them, none of this could be done.

CHAPTER 1

Orienting Perspectives

What does it mean when educators talk about the relationship between theory and practice? Can we separate the two? This book offers a foundation in current theoretical frameworks in literacy and considers their relevance for classroom practice. We present theoretical frameworks for understanding literacy that take the position that literacy is grounded in social, cultural, historical and political practices (Barton and Hamilton, 1998; Gee, 1996; Kress, 2003; Lankshear and Knobel, 2003a; Street, 1984; 2004). We argue that the dominant framework currently in place in schools originates from the discipline of educational psychology and translates into reductionist pedagogical frames which in turn engender teacher-centered, transmission models of curriculum. We present these alternative frameworks in order to expand teachers' thinking about what might be possible in classrooms and to help them to develop further their theoretical basis for practice. Novice researchers may also find this book useful as they explore theoretical foundations for literacy research.

This first chapter discusses the role of theoretical frameworks, or sets of propositions (Barton and Hamilton, 1998), in teaching and learning and the need to draw on multidisciplinary frameworks in order to first understand literacy teaching and learning and then to construct meaningful pedagogy. In the following chapters, we unpack four theoretical frameworks separately, outline them in detail, describe a classroom context which is informed by a particular theoretical model and interview leading scholars whose work has informed these particular theories. We then consider how teachers may use any or all of these theoretical models as they construct curricula and pedagogy, drawing from multidisciplinary perspectives. Finally, we discuss the implications of this multidisciplinary, social practice framework for teacher education and literacy research. First, however, this introductory chapter outlines the underlying definitions of literacy and learning that will guide the theoretical frameworks discussed.

THEORY AND PRACTICE QUESTIONS

As we began thinking about this book, we realized that students in our teacher education courses are sometimes overwhelmed by the readings we assign in our graduate programmes and by trying to make sense of literacy theory. In particular, they are trying to make links to what they call 'practice'. We occasionally face comments like, 'The theory is great, but what does this look like in a classroom?' Reading articles that report on detailed ethnographic research undertaken in classrooms help them to make some connections, but students may still feel like there is a separation. Our goal here is to illustrate the inseparability of theory and practice, to disrupt the idea of separation altogether. Scribner adds important insight into this problem:

> What a theory 'means' for practice cannot be read off from texts of the theory. Notions such as 'translating theory into practice' or 'applying theory to practice' are based on the contrary assumption. They imply, erroneously in my opinion, that grand theoretical propositions can be directly converted into methods for transforming established practices in the contingent here-and-now. (Scribner, 1990: 91)

Thus, thinking there is a simple transfer from theory to practice misunderstands the nature of the relationship. We are making the case here that theory is practice and practice is theorized as practice is transformed over time. As we discuss later in Chapter 5, we connect this idea to learning as changing participation. In other words, what teachers and students do is grounded in theories of literacy, learning, culture and history, and through participating in the practices of teaching and learning, those theories develop and change, in addition to the teachers and students themselves. Teaching and learning literacy is a mutually constituted process that changes over time. There is no direct 'how to' transfer, given that the relationship between theory and practice is so much more complex.

It is the processes involved in praxis that are important for educators to consider in terms of the development of a coherent framework for their teaching. Freire suggests that everyday human activity, 'consists of action and reflection: it is praxis; it is transformation of the world. And as praxis it requires theory to illuminate it' (Freire, 1972: 96). Therefore, there is not a linear relationship between theory and practice in that both inform and transform the other through a reiterative process of critical reflection and action. In this book, we feature four teachers and teacher-researchers whose work demonstrates this process: Lynn Gatto (Chapter 2), Vivian Vasquez (Chapter 3), Hilary Malden (Chapter 4), and Maryrita Maier (Chapter 5). We explore their classrooms and identify those features which reflect a particular theoretical framework. Although literacy education is informed by a wide array of theoretical paradigms, we have chosen just four because we believe that these four are important in considering the complexities of literacy education in the twenty-first century, yet they rarely feature in teacher education programs. These theoretical traditions are as follows:

1 New Literacy Studies: New Literacy Studies (NLS) offers a theoretical framework that assumes literacy is a critical social practice constructed in everyday interactions across local contexts. New Literacy Studies emphasizes literacy as a more complex social practice than mandated curricula and assessments address. We describe Lynn Gatto, a veteran teacher with more than 30 years' experience in urban schools, and her students in their elementary classroom in Rochester, New York. Brian Street visited Gatto's classroom while in Rochester and is thus a fitting NLS scholar for the interview that closes this chapter.

2 Critical literacy: critical literacy involves interrogating texts in terms of the power dynamics embedded within and reflected by them, in addition to positioning readers and authors as active agents in text creation and analysis. Although there has been a proliferation of writing on critical literacy, there are, as yet, few studies which illuminate this theoretical framework in action in primary classrooms. Vivian Vasquez and Barbara Comber are two scholars whose work has been important in pushing forward the boundaries of this field. It is appropriate, therefore, that the case study outlines Vasquez's practice when she was an elementary teacher and that we interview Barbara Comber about her reflections on this classroom practice.

3 New technologies and literacy: this theoretical framework draws on the work of the New London Group (1996) on multiliteracies, which attracted educators' attention to the way in which communicative modes were proliferating and changing due to advances in technology. Since then, the work of scholars such as Kress (2003) and Lankshear and Knobel (2003a) has been

important in developing our theoretical understanding of how technologies are transforming the epistemological and ontological foundations of literacy. In the chapter outlining this theoretical ground, we feature the classroom practice of Hilary Malden in England and interview Michele Knobel and Colin Lankshear in order to reflect on the issues raised by this case study. At various points in the book, we use the term 'techno-literacy' as a shorthand means of referring to the literacy practices which involve, or are shaped by, new technologies. However, we acknowledge that this theoretical paradigm cannot be encapsulated by a single term, and we are aware that the adoption of a phrase such as this can place an overemphasis on the technologies themselves rather than the textual practices they engender.

4   Sociocultural-historical theory: this theoretical framework challenges traditional definitions of learning as the transmission of knowledge. From this perspective, learning is defined as changing participation in culturally valued activity with more expert others. Using the case study of a 28-year veteran first grade teacher, Maryrita Maier, we illustrate how teaching and learning from a sociocultural-historical perspective can be realized. We end by interviewing Barbara Rogoff.

These chapters offer insights into how teachers can plan and organize class-rooms so that complex theoretical models of literacy inform their practice, rather than regurgitate mandated (or, in some countries, commercial) curricula that usually embed more traditional approaches to the teaching and learning of language and literacy.

TRADITIONAL APPROACHES TO LITERACY EDUCATION

For many years, literacy education has been grounded in a cognitive psychological approach in which attention is paid to individual development along a carefully traced trajectory. This model can be seen in many contemporary curriculum frameworks, such as the *National Literacy Strategy* (DfEE, 1998) in England and the No Child Left Behind (NCLB) Act in the United States. In the *National Literacy Strategy Framework for Teaching* (DfEE, 1998), for example, skills, knowledge and understanding for reading and writing are set out in a linear model in which children are introduced to specific concepts at specific ages. Such a model assumes that children progress in similar ways and acquire specific skills in sequence. This model of reading education draws heavily from the work of cognitive psychologists who proposed stage models of reading acquisition, researchers such as Ehri (1987; 1995). In the Framework's additional guidance on the teaching of phonics, the influence of these cognitive-psychological models can be seen in detail by examining the way in which it is suggested children are taught phoneme-grapheme relationships. In *Progression in Phonics* (DfES, 1999) teachers are advised to teach phonics in seven sequential steps. Apart from Step 1, which suggests that children should be taught 'general sounds, speech sounds and patterns', all the steps identify a specific range of phonemes which children should be taught in that step. This is one example of the way in which traditional approaches to the teaching of reading and writing conceptualize literacy as if it consists of a set of discrete skills that can be taught in isolation. Individual, repeated practice of these skills is at the heart of much of the pedagogy associated with these approaches.

Once a progression in skills, knowledge and understanding is established, it is a small step to begin to normalize development through this progression. In this way, children who do not acquire these skills, knowledge and understanding at the same rate as peers are soon identified as inadequate in some way. When this happens with whole groups of children who share socioeconomic backgrounds, then the creation of a deficit model is quickly established. In the latter half of the twentieth century, a range of terms were utilized to identify groups of children who were underachieving, and who may be living with poverty. One popular phrase to emerge was 'at risk': children who originated from homes in which poverty was a feature of life were seen to be at risk of failure. However, this phrase only serves to pathologize particular groups of children, and means that educators focus on the perceived negative aspects of their experiences rather than looking at what the children bring to classrooms and how classrooms can adapt to reflect and build on these experiences (Carrington and Luke, 2003). In addition, traditional models of literacy come to be associated with the 'normally developing' child who, it is assumed, lives in a family which should support the child's development through the provision of particular resources and literacy practices. Thus white, middle-class norms become established as the desirable literacy experiences which all children should enjoy, and intervention programs are then needed to ensure that parents of children living in so-called 'at risk' families are taught how to support their child's literacy development toward this one predetermined end. This, unfortunately, is a model of literacy education which pervades the developed world and creates misunderstandings about the needs of specific groups of learners (Gee, 2004).

■ BERNSTEIN'S CONCEPTUAL TOOLS

In any analysis of traditional approaches to literacy education, the conceptual tools offered by Basil Bernstein (1974; 2000) are useful. In order to analyze the structure of curricular and pedagogic discourse, Bernstein developed the concepts of 'classification' and 'frame' (Bernstein, 1974). 'Classification' was a term Bernstein used to describe the degree of boundary maintenance between subject matter. Strong classification suggests clear boundaries between subject matter. 'Frame', on the other hand, refers to the pedagogical context in which knowledge is transmitted. Strong framing means that the content, organization and delivery of what is to be transmitted is not in the control of the teacher or pupil (Bernstein, 1974: 205–6). In addition, Bernstein argues that out-of-school knowledge clearly has no place in school because of this framing and asks:

> how strong are the frames of educational knowledge in relation to experiential, community based non-school knowledge? I suggest that the frames of the collection code, very early in the child's life, socialize him (sic) into knowledge frames which discourage connections with everyday realities, or that there is a highly selective screening of the connection. Through such socialization, the pupil soon learns what of the outside may be brought into the pedagogical frame. (Bernstein, 1974: 215)

Moreover, when the frame of educational knowledge in school is relaxed to include knowledge from the community, it is often only used in classes with underachievers, 'The weakening of this frame occurs usually with the less "able" children whom we have given up educating' (Bernstein, 1974: 215). Classification and framing provide a strong model for analysing the way in which the education system privileges some forms of literacy knowledge and styles of pedagogy over others. Part of the way in which classification (Bernstein, 1974) works is to outline what constitutes knowledge in any particular subject. Most mandated curricula present strong classification and framing of knowledge (Bernstein, 1974) in relation to the primary literacy curriculum (see Marsh, 2004a for an analysis of the National Literacy Strategy's framing of knowledge in England). Moreover, the selection of knowledge in most curricula reflects hegemonic interests and thus can be seen as an example of symbolic violence (Bourdieu and Passeron, 1977). The selection of texts that constitute the primary canon is usually based on the tastes and experiences of a specific section of society, a section which possesses sufficient cultural, economic and symbolic capital in the field of education to assert its authority. In this book, you will see examples of classrooms in which this traditional framing of knowledge has been challenged in order to incorporate children's out-of-school interests in meaningful ways that counteract the marginalization of students' language and literacy practices. The teachers featured in these pages have finely tuned their praxis by reflecting carefully on the way that theory and practice relate to each other in their classrooms. In this way, they have been able to identify those traditional literacy practices that are privileged by compulsory curriculum frameworks and to find ways in which such strong classification and framing of knowledge can be contested.

A further concept of Bernstein's which relates to traditional approaches to the teaching of literacy is that of visible and invisible pedagogies. An invisible pedagogy 'is realized through weak classification and weak frames. Visible pedagogies are realized through strong classification and strong frames' (Bernstein, 1977: 511). In defining the concept of invisible pedagogy, Bernstein outlines a vision of classrooms:

1 *Where the control of the teacher over the child is implicit rather than explicit.*

2 *Where, ideally, the teacher arranges the context which the child is expected to rearrange and explore.*

3 *Where within this arranged context, the child apparently has wide powers over what he (sic) selects, over how he structures, and over the timescale of his activities.*

4 *Where the child apparently regulates his own movements and social relationships.*

5 *Where there is a reduced emphasis upon the transmission and acquisition of specific skills.*

6 *Where the criteria for evaluating the pedagogy are multiple and diffuse and not so easily measured. (1977: 511)*

In contrast, classrooms which utilize a model of visible pedagogy are ones in which teachers have explicit control. The model of teaching here is one of transmission – the teachers possess the knowledge, which they have to impart to pupils in a regulated manner. However, the empirical basis of Bernstein's analysis is not clear and this is especially noticeable in the case of invisible pedagogies, which he suggests reflect the pedagogy of infant classrooms in England in the 1960s. It is difficult, in fact, to find evidence that this was ever the case to the extent that Bernstein suggests. Nevertheless, the invisible/visible pedagogies dichotomy is a useful theoretical tool in that it enables an analysis of the ways in which the pedagogy of literacy teaching is more visible in many state and national curricula that outline explicitly the knowledge which children should acquire for: 'the more specific the criteria, the more explicit the manner of their transmission, the more visible the pedagogy' (Bernstein, 1977: 511). Bernstein's work is thus predicated on a set of binaries that can be summarized as shown in Table 1.1.

Table 1.1 Bernstein's binaries

Strong classification	Weak classification
Clear boundaries between subjects	Weak boundaries between subjects
Strong framing	**Weak framing**
Weak control by teacher and learner over pedagogy	Strong control by teacher and learner over pedagogy
Visible pedagogy	**Invisible pedagogy**
Results from strong classification and framing	Results from weak classification and framing

We would suggest that traditional approaches to the teaching and learning of literacy would align with the categories in the left-hand column, in which the skills, knowledge and understanding that children are to acquire are set out in an explicit manner, and the pedagogical approaches leave little room for teacher and pupil autonomy. The emphasis is on ensuring that pupils progress along a predetermined path and on forging classroom practice which is predicated on individualized learning.

KEY CONCEPTS

In contrast to traditional transmission models that focus on individualized learning, the classrooms featured in this book reflect theoretical models of literacy which place less emphasis on the individual. Instead, they focus on literacy as a social practice and work on the premise that knowledge about literacy is socially constructed. In this model, discourse communities within classrooms become an important feature of pedagogical approaches as the social nature of learning is emphasized and learning is recognized as changing participation. In the following section, the key concepts of 'learning as changing participation', 'literacy as a social practice' and 'discourse' are discussed, given their recurrence throughout the book.

▓ LEARNING AS CHANGING PARTICIPATION

Throughout the book, we focus on learning, using Rogoff's (2003) definition of learning as changing participation, discussed in Chapter 5. However,
using Rogoff's ideas often presents educators with a real challenge. Many
educators understand the idea of transmission models of learning and can
see, or at least begin to see, that simple transmission may be inadequate. In
addition, we understand acquisition theories of learning because we are
familiar with the idea of student-centered learning, especially in early childhood. It is more difficult for some educators to understand the kind of
learning-centered context that Rogoff (1994; 2003) describes. Larson finds
that telling the story of her daughter Anna's coffee adventure often helps
others begin to think about how people learn. Here's the story:

> When my oldest two children were 5 and 2, I was a single parent, working
> three jobs and getting my PhD at UCLA. I pretty much focused on routine to
> get things done. Every morning was the same. I got up before my kids, or at
> least they were getting dressed, playing or watching TV, so I could get their
> breakfast ready, pack their lunches, and make my coffee and toast. It was
> always the same. I would put cereal in their bowls and put milk in a child-
> sized jug on the table. I would make their lunches, sometimes while they ate
> breakfast, and always included a sandwich, a piece of fruit, a bag of chips,
> and a juice box and maybe a treat. I put the lunch box in front of each
> child's place at the table. I would grind my coffee beans and brew the coffee.
> I usually make it pretty strong, in fact so strong that it's a family joke.
> Anyway, I put in my toast. I waited a minute before putting on butter and
> jam, because I don't like the butter to melt all the way. I prepared my coffee
> with one sweetener packet and some non-fat milk. I would drink the coffee
> and eat the toast while they finished their breakfast.
> One Saturday morning early, I was awakened by the smell of coffee. My first
> thought was, 'Oh, oh, this could be good thing or this could be a very bad
> thing.' Who the heck was making coffee? It had to be one of the kids. I went
> into the kitchen and my jaw dropped. Anna, then 5, had prepared breakfast,
> made coffee, and packed lunches. Not just any way though. She had done it
> exactly like me. The cereal bowls were full and on the table at place settings.
> The milk was poured into the child-sized jug. The lunch boxes contained
> sandwiches, a piece of fruit, a bag of chips, and a juice box (never mind that
> it was Saturday). My coffee was ground, brewed, and in a cup with sweet-
> ener and milk. My toast was toasted, buttered and jellied just how I like it. I
> was speechless. The only thing she did 'wrong' if you could call it that was to
> turn off the coffee machine so the coffee was cold. I didn't say a word. It
> seemed remarkably unimportant.

How does this relate to learning as changing participation? Anna did not learn this by me teaching her in a lesson. I did not instruct her. Frankly, I didn't even scaffold her participation in this activity by gradually giving her things to do. She learned by observing and by participating peripherally in the morning routine. Her participation changed pretty quickly, but it is a good illustration of the theory to me.

One year, a student in Larson's graduate class said, 'So she learned how to make coffee. Big deal. How does this apply to learning to read? Or to becoming literate?' Good questions. Students in the class began to talk about how they learned to cook, knit, ride a bike, or to be a woman or man. Discussion centered on the question, 'If we learn to ride a bike by riding a bike with the help of someone who already knows how or we learn to knit by watching our mothers or grandmothers, getting samplers to practice and sitting with her as we try our own piece, getting help as we need it, why do we change the context for learning so dramatically in schools?' It seems like common sense to think that participation changes over time as expertise and ability increases. So, if people learn by participating in culturally valued activities, what are we doing in schools? In what are students participating and for what purpose? In the case studies foregrounded in this book, we present examples of classrooms in which children participate in meaningful 'communities of practice' (Lave and Wenger, 1991) and where learning can be clearly seen as changing participation. Literacy therefore becomes a social practice and, in the next section, we move on to consider this notion.

LITERACY AS A SOCIAL PRACTICE

The idea that everyday reality is socially constructed stems from the work of Berger and Luckman (1966) in the field of sociology of knowledge. In this view, knowledge (and reality) is an ongoing, dialectical construction of worldviews. Individuals and groups construct worldviews (everyday realities) in interaction with society. These constructed worldviews are mediated by language and culture in an ongoing process of identity construction. In other words, the meaning of everyday concepts such as gender and teaching are highly contingent on social, cultural, historical, and political processes. A social practice model of literacy is built on the recognition that literacy is also constructed in everyday practices. As Barton and Hamilton suggest:

Literacy is primarily something people do; it is an activity, located in the space between thought and text. Literacy does not just reside in people's heads as a set of skills to be learned, and it does not just reside on paper, captured as texts to be analyzed. Like all human activity, literacy is essentially social, and it is located in the interaction between people. (1998: 3)

In this model, literacy is not a discrete set of skills to be acquired, but situated within specific contexts and shaped by social interaction. Context becomes particularly important when we consider how space is socially as well as materially constituted (Sheehy and Leander, 2004: 3) and, in some of the case studies, examples of the way literacy is shaped by both specific participants in a literacy event and the context itself are presented.

A key concept in relation to literacy as a social practice, that of the dualistic positioning of autonomous and ideological models of literacy (Street, 1995), is discussed further in Chapter 2, but we will introduce it briefly here. An autonomous model of literacy is one in which literacy is defined as a discrete set of skills that can be taught in similar ways across varying contexts; it is value-free literacy and, as such, can be applied in analogous ways despite the very different needs and experiences of learners.

Alternatively, an ideological model of literacy is one in which its constitution as a social practice is recognized. In this model, literacy is shaped by particular social, cultural, economic and political contexts and is always ideological, that is, always carries particular meanings and is imbued with power (Street, 1995). In relation to the discussions we have had thus far with regard to literacy education, we would argue that it is generally an autonomous model of literacy which underpins the construction of curricula in many countries. In the case studies presented in this book, ideological models of literacy pervade the teachers' pedagogical practices.

As we try to understand literacy as a social practice, we necessarily need to understand the role language plays in literacy learning and use. What is language? Is it just talk? What do scholars means when they talk about discourse? We draw from several fields to articulate what we mean when we discuss language, talk, and discourse. Engaging with research in linguistic anthropology, we define talk as social action in which participants in an interaction co-construct meaning (Duranti, 1997; Goodwin, 1990). If talk is connected to social action and meaning-making, then how is it different from how current scholars are defining discourse?

DISCOURSE

The distinction between talk and discourse is echoed in Gee's (1999) notion of little 'd' and big 'D' D/discourse. Discourse with a 'big D' represents the various culturally organized ways of acting and being in the world, or 'forms of life', that are enacted, reproduced, or transformed through language in use, or what Gee calls discourse with a 'little d'. Similarly, Ochs (1988: 8) defines discourse as a 'set of norms, preferences, and expectations relating linguistic structures to context, which speaker-hearers draw on and modify in producing and interpreting language in context'. We use discourse here to describe what Bakhtin (1981; 1986) terms a social language that understands the utterance to be an active representative of the voice or voices that are reflected in and produced from an organized social context, such as schools and classrooms (Larson and Peterson, 2003).

Further, we use definitions of discourse in critical discourse analysis to explore how discourse in local sites (for example, classrooms) and in larger social structures constructs and positions and is constructed and positioned by human subjects (Foucault, 1972; Luke, 1995). Critical discourse analysts acknowledge the dialectical relationship between discourse in use and the larger social structures, each constituting and transforming the other through social interactions (Fairclough, 1992; Luke, 1995).

We bring these concepts together to think about literacy discourses as representative of a group who has texts, practices, ways of knowing and being in common, collective purposes and ways of socializing new members (Barton, 1994) (for example, teachers, administrators). Applying this idea more specifically to learning to read, Gee states:

> Learning to read a text of a given type in a given way, then, requires scaffolded socialization into the groups and social practices that make a text of this type to be read in this way. Being able to read a text of a given type a given way requires that one is a member of such social groups and is able to engage in their practices. And here is the final rub: those practices, even as they recruit written texts centrally, rarely involve only written text. They involve ways of talking and listening, acting and interacting, thinking and believing, and feeling and valuing, as well. All this – types of text, ways of reading them, social groups and their practices that go beyond writing – is what falls under the notion of 'something' when we talk about reading something *and have to say what that something is. To leave the something off, which is what the Academy's report ultimately does, is to leave out language, learning, development, society, culture, and history. It is, in the end, ironically, to leave out reading. (2001: 17, emphases in original)

The concept of D/discourse applies to classrooms when we begin to think about how language is used in everyday classroom interaction and ask: what are the consequences of this use on literacy learning? To begin to understand the role of language in literacy learning, we draw on the extensive literature in classroom discourse. Mehan's (1979) now famous study of Courtney Cazden and her subsequent book on classroom discourse

(1988) forged new ground in understanding how language works to enable or constrain participation in learning. Gutierrez (1993) articulated a range of discourse patterns, building on this earlier work. Nystrand (1997) studied hundreds of classrooms in order to document the relationship of authentic discourse to learning. Green and Harker (1988) provide painstaking analyses of moment-to-moment classroom interaction that illustrates the nature of learning in interaction. Recent work by Bloome et al. (2005) takes a microanalytic view of discourse analysis that affords key insights into literacies in use. These studies form the foundation of classroom discourse studies.

Of particular note here is the identification of what Mehan (1979) called the IRE pattern. IRE, or initiation–response–evaluation, is the dominant discourse structure in classrooms. In this pattern, teachers typically ask a question for which they already have the answer. A student responds and the teacher evaluates that response. For example:

- Teacher: What's the capital of New York?

- Student: Albany

- Teacher: Good!

We all recognize this interaction. It is probably how we remember our own experiences with classroom interaction. What we may not remember are the consequences of this pattern on our learning.

We use Gutierrez's (1993) framework here to illustrate the connection of classroom discourse structure to theoretical frameworks. In this work, Gutierrez articulated three types of structures: recitation, responsive, and responsive collaborative. Table 1.2 briefly summarizes the categories described by Gutierrez.

The 'recitation' model relates most closely to traditional approaches to teaching, as discussed earlier in this chapter. The responsive/collaborative model underpins much of the classroom practice outlined in this book, as will be illustrated in the case studies.

Throughout this introductory chapter, we have considered a number of concepts that have been presented as discreet binaries that may be interpreted as oppositional or mutually exclusive: strong/weak classification and framing; visible/invisible pedagogies; recitation/responsive and collaborative structures; autonomous/ideological models of literacy; teaching as transmission or transformation. Traditional models of literacy education have been framed as reflecting one particular set of these binaries, those

Table 1.2 Classroom discourse categories

Recitation	Responsive	Responsive/collaborative
■ Strict IRE discourse pattern	■ More relaxed IRE discourse pattern (that is, more student responses between initiation and evaluation)	■ Boundaries of participation significantly relaxed; chained utterances (responses build on previous utterances) contribute to the construction of shared understanding
■ Teacher selection of speakers		
■ Little or no recognition of student self-selection		
■ High frequency of teacher-selected topics and subtopics	■ Teacher dominates speaker selection, however, there is increased opportunity for student self-selection	■ Teacher frames and facilitates activity but keeps contributions and turn selection to a minimum; student self-selection or select others
■ Limited student responses to teacher-generated questions (one word); little encouragement of elaborated response and minimal expansion of student's responses	■ Some incorporation of student generated sub-topics into class discussion	
	■ Longer student responses with some encouragement by the teacher for elaboration	■ Frequent instances of student topic expansion and incorporation of these topics into discussion by both the teacher and students; shared negotiation of ongoing sub-topics
■ Teacher-initiated 'test-like' questions for which there is generally one correct answer; implied goal is getting *the* right answer	■ Teacher initiates questions for which there are several possible answers; implied goal combines getting the correct answer and developing shared understanding	
■ Minimal opportunity for all class members to participate	■ Increased opportunities for more students to participate	■ Elaborated student responses with greater number of students participating
		■ Teacher- and student-generated questions for which there are no specific correct answers, including questions emerging from previous student responses
		■ Implied goal is struggle for intersubjectivity (shared knowledge)

which reflect restricted notions of curriculum and pedagogy. However, we would not want to argue that the categories outlined above are oppositional in a simplistic manner. Instead, the development of curriculum and pedagogy takes place along a continuum in which each of the categories stand at either end, as represented in Figure 1.1.

Transmission models of teaching	Transformational models of teaching
Strong classification	Weak classification
Strong framing	Weak framing
Visible pedagogies	Invisible pedagogies
Autonomous literacy	Ideological literacy
Recitation structures	Responsive/collaborative structures

Figure 1.1 Continua of positions

Consistent with our discussion of a multidisciplinary theoretical framework in Chapter 6, teachers' practice may be placed on different parts of these continua at different times, depending on the context/purposes, and we suggest that whilst one might want to work primarily on the right-hand side, there may be specific lessons/sequences of lessons which demand a different approach. Good teachers are not hide-bound by rules and restrictions, but make sensitive judgments about what is required in any one set of circumstances.

So far, we have considered various theoretical approaches to understanding literacy curriculum and pedagogy. However, this book does not focus solely on issues of praxis; we also consider a number of these theoretical frameworks in relation to literacy research. In the final section in this chapter, we consider briefly the role of theory in research.

THE ROLE OF THEORY IN RESEARCH

Understanding where a theoretical framework 'fits' in relation to theories of being (ontology), theories of knowledge (epistemology), analytic framework and research questions is not a straightforward process. Figure 1.2 presents one way to think about the role theory plays in these processes.

This model might suggest that this process is a linear one: the researcher identifies research questions based on her or his ontological and epistemological understandings, determines where the research is to be located along

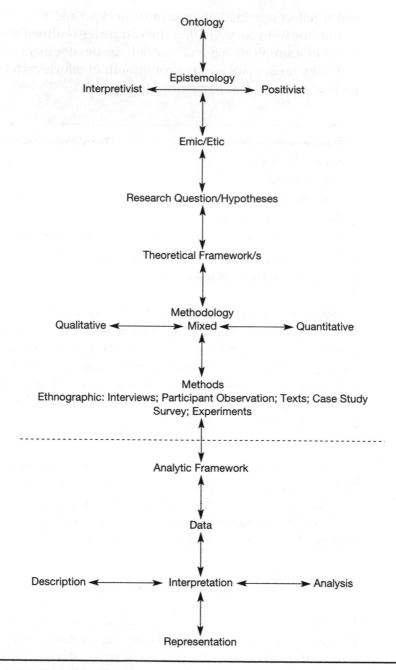

Ontology

Epistemology

Interpretivist ◄─────────────────► Positivist

Emic/Etic

Research Question/Hypotheses

Theoretical Framework/s

Methodology

Qualitative ◄──────► Mixed ◄──────► Quantitative

Methods
Ethnographic: Interviews; Participant Observation; Texts; Case Study
Survey; Experiments

Analytic Framework

Data

Description ◄──────► Interpretation ◄──────► Analysis

Representation

Figure 1.2 Locating Theory
(adapted from Brian Street's PhD Methodological Approach Research Seminar, King's College, London)

an interpretivist–positivist continuum and decides whether an emic (insider) or etic (outsider) perspective is to be adopted, depending on the particular issue/problem to be researched. The research questions or hypotheses are then identified and the theoretical underpinning to this work is developed. Methodological approaches and choices of methods are then driven by the previous considerations. An analytic framework is applied to the data and subsequent analysis of the data is then represented by the researcher in some form, for example, in a research report, dissertation or thesis.

However, the process of research is never that linear, and theory is not simply inserted at a convenient point along this track. It is important to view this figure as representative of recursive and continuous processes that are inextricably linked. In other words, the research question/s, theoretical framework, methodology, analyses are mutually constituted over the course of the study, although researchers commonly 'start' with the research question. For example, you may believe that humans are social beings (ontological position) and that knowledge is socially constructed (epistemology) and you may have a research question which focuses on the social construction of literacy. Given this focus, the multidisciplinary frameworks described in this book would all work well in helping to 'see' the data you collect. One might wish to work with the different models as distinct conceptualizations, or draw from each as best fits the research questions and the data. In Chapter 6, we consider how the conceptual models of literacy outlined in this book may work together or separately in issues relating to praxis and research.

CONCLUSION

In this introductory chapter, we have suggested that traditional approaches to literacy education are located within cognitive psychological models in their emphasis on individualized learning and normalized learning trajectories. In addition, we have drawn from the work of Bernstein (1974; 2000) to argue that these traditional models impart strong classification and framing, as well as embed restrictive pedagogical approaches, such as the recitation structure (see Table 1.2), in classroom practices. In the following chapters, you will find classrooms that have rejected these constraining models of practice and, instead, embraced a range of curricula and pedagogical approaches that foster collaborative learning and recognize the variety of strategies and resources students bring to classrooms. Next, we move on to examine closely the theoretical principles which underpin the New Literacy Studies.

CHAPTER 2

New Literacy Studies

The goal of this chapter is to outline what has come to be known as the New Literacy Studies (Gee, 1996; Street, 1993), or NLS for short, and to offer a glimpse into one classroom that will illustrate what NLS might look like in practice. We are responding to a perceived gap between what NLS research has to offer and what teachers do. Sometimes, novice and experienced teachers complain that 'academics' talk about theory but do not understand life on the ground in the classroom. One of the basic tenets of NLS is to deeply understand everyday life, including life in classrooms, in order to construct meaningful contexts for literacy learning. We argue here that NLS helps us understand that literacy learning does not simply occur in formal or informal settings, or in or out of school, but also occurs in-between in everyday interaction as tools for building and maintaining social relations.

HISTORICAL GROUND

To understand current conceptions of NLS, it is helpful to examine key historical points[1]. Literacy scholars established a body of work beginning in the late 1970s and early 1980s that described literacy as inextricably linked to social practices of literacy in use and challenged traditional reading and writing pedagogies (Graff, 1979; Heath, 1983; Scribner and Cole, 1981; Street, 1984). We focus on three key studies in this brief overview that point to significant shifts in thinking about literacy. We ground the theoretical overview in a classroom case study, followed by an interview with Brian Street.

The shift to understanding the practices of literacy in everyday life began to occur with the publication of Scribner and Cole's landmark study of Vai literacy (1981). In that study, Scribner and Cole argued that traditional psychological correlations between literacy and cognitive ability were overstated, if not unfounded. They found that the Vai used multiple literacy practices as means to accomplish social and cultural ends in everyday life, and that literacy did not necessarily link to cognitive ability. School literacy was linked to performance on school-related tasks and assessments (Cole, 1996). As a result of this work, we came to understand that literacy is not simply an individual cognitive activity, but is a communicative tool for different social groups with social rules about who can produce and use particular literacies for particular social purposes (Barton and Hamilton, 1998).

LITERACY EVENTS AND PRACTICES

In *Ways With Words*, Shirley Brice Heath established the concept of literacy events in her extensive ethnography of literacy in three communities in the Piedmont Carolinas. Heath's work is widely cited and described in the literature, and there is no need to do so again here. Instead, we will focus on the concepts of literacy events (Heath, 1983) and literacy practices (Street, 1995) as key tools in the development of literacy competence across communities of use. Heath (1983) defines a literacy event as an occasion where written text and talk around that text constructs interpretations, extensions and meanings. This concept emerged in the analysis of ten years of data and is consistent with Scribner and Cole's findings about uses of literacy. Heath found that written text played a significant but diverse role in the practices of everyday life. Each community used language and literacy for different purposes and different audiences.

Street takes the idea a bit further when he describes the social and linguistic practices that encompass literacy events. He argues that:

> the concept of literacy practices is pitched at a higher level of abstraction and refers to both behaviour and the social and cultural conceptualizations that give meaning to the uses of reading and/or writing. Literacy practices incorporate not only 'literacy events', as empirical occasions to which literacy is integral, but also folk models of those events and the ideological preconceptions that underpin them. (1995: 2)

For example, in many middle-class families, making a shopping list with a family member is a literacy event, whereas shopping is a social practice within which the use of a shopping list is one part. There are other literacy events in shopping (reading nutrition labels, identifying products, and so on). School has its own literacy events and practices that are based on what Street (1995) has called autonomous definitions of literacy; we discuss this concept next.

AUTONOMOUS AND IDEOLOGICAL LITERACY

Brian Street's (1993) cross-cultural ethnographies of literacy are another key foundation of NLS. Of interest to us in this chapter is his concept of autonomous and ideological definitions of literacy. Rather than being two opposing views, it is most helpful to think about autonomous and ideological definitions as being points on a continuum of definitions. On one end, autonomous models define literacy as a unified set of neutral skills that can be applied equally across all contexts (Street, 1995). From this perspective, there is no need to adjust instruction for different contexts of use or diverse learners. On the other end, ideological models define literacy as a social practice grounded in social, historical, cultural and political contexts of use. In this view, the nature and meaning of literacy are constructed in the specific social practices of participants in particular cultural settings for particular purposes. Thus, literacy is more than acquiring content but, in addition, locates reading and writing in the social and linguistic practices that give them meaning (Street, 1995).

To be more specific, autonomous models of literacy are based on a reductionist definition of literacy rooted in western schooling. These school-based concepts of literacy are held as a standard definition of literate competence across contexts. In other words, universalistic conceptions of literacy put forward in autonomous models assume text has meanings that are independent of its context of use. New Literacy Studies claims that texts do not have uses independent of the social meanings and purposes people construct (Barton and Hamilton, 1998). Furthermore, autonomous definitions associated with school can suppress students under the ideology and social control of dominant groups, preventing a critical analysis of their social and political contexts (see Chapter 3 for discussion of critical literacy). Thus, if literacy is represented as a context-neutral skill, then it fulfills the political purposes of those in power to maintain a position of superiority by marginalizing other forms of literate knowledge (Street, 1984), specifically the rich and varied practices students bring to the classroom.

An ideological view of literacy assumes that literacy is a set of social practices that are historically situated, highly dependent on shared cultural understandings and inextricably linked to power relations in any setting (Gee, 1996; Irvine and Larson, 2001; Street, 1995). Literacy is intimately tied to contexts of use or what people *do* with literacy in formal and informal settings, both inside and outside school. Literacy is not just reading and writing English text (in English dominant settings), but is a multimodal social practice with specific affordances in different contexts (Kress, 2003). From this perspective, social and linguistic practices are mutually constituted within past and present power relations among people who write and read to accomplish social goals. In this framework, the context is constituted by local, culturally specific practices that outline who has access to learning to read, and who writes which kinds of texts for which purposes.

IMPLICATIONS FOR CLASSROOMS

What does all this complexity mean for classrooms? On the one hand, it seems like common sense to think of literacy as what people do with text broadly defined. On the other hand, however, what is a teacher to do with a more complex understanding of literacy, especially in the current political context of high stakes accountability that is based on an autonomous definition? One way we thought might be a helpful tool for thinking about NLS and classroom practice is to use workshop approaches to teaching literacy (Atwell, 1998; Calkins, 1994; Graves, 1983) as a heuristic for discussing pedagogical implications. Readers' and writers' workshop is a familiar pedagogical model for teachers. The literature in this field has a tendency to leave out explicit theoretical articulation (Larson and Peterson, 2003). We believe workshop pedagogy and NLS are theoretically consistent and, thus, a nice starting point for discussing the theory/practice relationship.

CONNECTING NLS TO WORKSHOP PEDAGOGY

Writers' workshop works on the assumption that students will learn to write like real writers do. Typically, 'real' writers are defined as professional authors. Through author studies, modeling, conferences and sharing texts, students learn how people who are writers compose and publish text. New Literacy Studies argues that all writing is real writing, and that professional authors are not the only models of authentic texts. The task is for teachers to see themselves as writers and readers and move away from focusing exclusively on professional literacies to unpack how people use literacy in everyday life, including professionally.

Teachers need to ask themselves: what are my literacy practices? How do I write? How and what do I read? What kinds of things do I write/read? When? For what purposes? How do my students use literacy in their communities? When? For what purposes? Answering these questions forms the foundation of transforming classroom literacy practices using an NLS perspective. Curriculum design thus includes a deep understanding of teachers' and students' local literacy practices. Once teachers understand their own practices they can take that knowledge to what they do in their classrooms. Furthermore, NLS nudges the readers' and writers' workshop framework to move beyond professional and/or creative writing so teachers can see ways to construct authentic reading and writing pedagogy based on everyday practices.

As we discussed earlier, one form of literacy, an autonomous or school-based definition, has come to dominate literacy practices in contemporary schooling. Using NLS as a framework, Street (1995: 106) claims that through a process he calls the 'pedagogization of literacy', objectified conceptions of literacy are naturalized in practice (for example, no one questions their origins or purposes anymore). Pedagogization is defined as the socially constructed link between institutionalized processes of teaching and learning and literacy. By reducing literacy to a neutral set of reading and writing skills, literacy is defined apart from social context and becomes, then, a 'content to be taught through authority structures whereby pupils learned the proper roles and identities they were to carry into the wider world' (Street, 1995: 118). In other words, students learn the D/discourses (Gee, 1996) required to conform to school practices and purposes, and are not considered legitimate contributors to those practices and purposes.

To what does this kind of socialization lead? If unquestioned, a school-based definition of literacy can lead to simple consumption and implementation of packaged literacy programs (Larson, 2001) and a belief that the texts themselves can teach literacy (Shannon, 1992), instead of understanding that literacy learning is a profoundly social process. While we elaborate this point much more in Chapter 5, it is important to say now that to move beyond autonomous literacy that engenders transmission of static content, we need contexts for learning where students can actively share in the construction of the goals, purposes and practices of literacies in the classroom.

UNDERSTANDING LITERACY AS SOCIAL PRACTICE

Building on Barton and Hamilton (1998), we propose a set of NLS propositions in Table 2.1 to use as a base upon which we might begin to rethink traditional classroom literacy practices and as a framework to inform literacy research.

Table 2.1 Principles of New Literacy Studies

1. Literacy practices and events are always situated in social, cultural, historical, and political relationships and are embedded in structures of power (Barton, 1994; Barton and Hamilton, 1998; Cope and Kalantzis, 2000; Street, 1995; 1997; 1999).

2. Being literate involves being communicatively competent across multiple discourse communities (Barton, 1994; Gee, 1996; 2001). Literacy practices and events are embedded in Discourses (Gee, 1996; 2001; Gee, et al., 1996) and are integrated into people's everyday lived practices on multiple levels (Gee et al., 1996).

3. Social inequalities based on race, class, gender, ability, sexual orientation, and so on structure access to participation in literacy events and practices (Barton and Hamilton, 1998).

4. Literacy practices involve the social regulation of text, that is who has access to them and who can produce them (Barton and Hamilton, 1998: 17; Luke, 1994).

5. The impact of new information and communication technologies changes the nature of literacy and thus what needs to be learned (Kress, 2003; Lankshear and Knobel, 2003a).

6. The changing nature of work also demands a new view of language that is multimodal (Kress, 2003) and more complex than traditional conceptions. The notion of multiliteracies emerges (Cope and Kalantzis, 2000). In other words, people use different kinds of literacy across domains of life (discourse communities).

7. Literacy practices are purposeful and embedded in broader social goals and cultural practices (Barton and Hamilton, 1998: 7; Gee, 2001; Street, 1995).

8. Literacy practices change, and new ones are frequently acquired through processes of informal learning and sense-making (Barton and Hamilton, 1998: 7).

The propositions in Table 2.1 are intimately connected and overlap in significant ways, and articulate how literacies are embedded in the practices of everyday life (de Certeau, 1984). From this perspective, we might think of school as one of the many kinds of practices people do in which literacy/literacies play a role. What are the pedagogical implications of these propositions? We attempt to make some claims in two ways. First, we briefly discuss some implications in the next section, followed by a detailed case example of one urban classroom.

CONNECTING NLS PROPOSITIONS TO CLASSROOM PRACTICES

The propositions discussed in the previous section help us to transform the teaching and learning of literacy from the unquestioned school-based concept to one that is grounded in authentic practices. If literacies are always situated in social, cultural, historical and political relationships, and are embedded in structures of power, then teachers need to get a clear understanding of both their literacy practices and the practices of the local community, including those of their students and families. Home visits that are conducted without negative assumptions about students may be an important research tool for teachers to understand their students' practices. Our case study teacher conducts home visits every summer before school begins and gives parents and/or caregivers a survey that asks about the child, the family and the literacy practices of the home and neighborhood, for example.

In order to facilitate communicative competence across multiple discourse communities, children need experiences participating in communities beyond their classroom and local community. The school field trip may be one way to expose children to different discourse communities; however, typical field trips are most often used as extensions of classroom activities (Larson, 2005). We will discuss another way to use field trips in the case study section of this chapter.

Social regulation of texts based on race, class, gender, ability, sexual orientation and other aspects of identity engenders unequal access to participation in literacy events and practices. Careful teacher self-reflection on both their ideological assumptions and pedagogical practices is key in ensuring that inequities of access and participation do not occur. Teacher research has been a fruitful resource (Lankshear and Knobel, 2004d). Our case study teacher uses strategies that include analyzing videotape of her practice, content analysis of student and teacher texts, and professional reading to counteract these processes. Chapter 3 describes how critical literacy may be an additional frame for teachers to use.

Understanding the purposeful nature of literacy practices and their connection to broader social goals and cultural practices means that school texts need to have real audiences and real purposes. Teachers need to move beyond literacy exercises (Edelsky, 1991) to authentic practices connected to broader social and cultural practices, beginning with the practices of their students and local communities. Students need to be a part of constructing the purposes of the activities they are asked to do. Students could identify an issue, local and/or global, and use literacy to effect change. For example, during a thematic unit on butterflies (Gatto, 2001) the students in our case study classroom read about the logging industry's destruction of the Monarch butterfly habitats in Mexico. They wrote letters to the Mexican government with alternative ideas.

Given that literacy practices change, sometimes rapidly, educators need flexibility and adaptability. Professional reading in the literacy field may be a valuable resource for teachers to be aware of new research and/or emerging practices that ought to be taken into account when developing curricula and may help avoid reducing literacy practices to school lessons. New Literacy Studies helps us see the process and consequences of this pedagogization and provides a valuable lens through which to understand the complex processes of teaching and learning literacy in new times.

IMPLICATIONS FOR RESEARCHING LITERACY

There is already a large and growing body of research from an NLS perspective, some of which we described here. In addition, there have been meaningful critiques that challenge NLS researchers to connect their ethnographic work to classrooms more explicitly (Street, 2005). Several key scholars are of particular note.

Colin Lankshear and Michelle Knobel are asking important and innovative questions in their current work (see Chapter 4 for further discussion). For example, an intriguing question they ask is, what's 'new' in new literacies (Lankshear and Knobel, 2003a)? Teacher education in particular has not kept up with what may be the implications of 'new' literacies on classroom practice. We still need to ask, how can New Literacy Studies help us to understand 'new' literacies in ways that do not reify or pedagogize them, thus taking the meaning out?

Research using NLS as a theoretical starting point necessitates an ideological definition of literacy (Street, 1995). When we conduct research, we are always researching 'something' for some purpose. New Literacy Studies describes that something in context-specific ways that does not imply universals and that complements collaborative research with teachers, students and community members, specifically through ethnography (Heath, 1983). Research on students as ethnographers of their own language and culture (Egan-Robertson and Bloome, 1998; Elsasser and Irvine, 1985; Irvine and Elsasser, 1988) offers additional resources for researching literacies in use from an NLS perspective.

CLASSROOM CASE STUDY: LYNN ASTARITO GATTO, ROCHESTER CITY SCHOOL DISTRICT, USA

My students understand that learning does not take place just in school; they leave my classroom with a passion for experiencing new places and meeting new people. (Lynn Gatto)

This section offers a detailed account of one urban classroom as an example of what NLS might look like when used explicitly by the teacher. The data for this description are taken from a long-term ethnography in Lynn Gatto's classroom conducted by Larson from 2000 to 2003. We present a brief description of Gatto, followed by an outline of her curriculum and pedagogy. We focus specifically on her field trip practices as key events that represent how NLS can foster student learning.

CONTEXT

Lynn Gatto has taught all grades at the elementary level in the Rochester City School District for over 30 years. She has received numerous local and national awards, including a 2001 Toyota Tapestry Award and the Presidential Award for Excellence in Science and Mathematics Teaching in 1997. Most recently, she was named the 2004 New York State Teacher of the Year. She is a national presenter at educational and research conferences and has published in teacher journals and in literacy research books (Gatto, 2001). She recently completed writing elementary science curriculum modules for a national publishing company. In addition to all of this, she is a doctoral student in the University of Rochester's Warner Graduate School of Education and Human Development.

Larson first met Gatto in her graduate education courses. The force of her personality and her convictions about teaching were immediately evident. It was not that she was particularly vocal in class discussion as much as she was so forceful when they talked one on one or with small groups of the other students Gatto knew. She was not a 'typical' veteran teacher attending graduate school, although she certainly had to make the transition from just talking about her classroom to thinking from a more analytic and theoretical frame. It seemed to take a shorter time than most in Larson's experience. Gatto appeared to recognize herself in the theories she was reading.

The confidence Gatto had in her own teaching took Larson by surprise at first. Larson had done a lot of research in the city school district by that point and she was starting to lose hope that there was meaningful literacy pedagogy happening in the city district. Her research had shown that the deficit model remained a strong influence on practice, to the detriment of student learning (Irvine and Larson, 2001; Larson, 2003; Larson and Irvine, 1999). Gatto's enthusiasm and dedication remained dominant in all interactions, however, and it became clear that she 'walked like she talked'. The examples she talked about and the connections she made to the research and theory they were discussing in coursework made sense.

PHYSICAL ENVIRONMENT AND RESOURCES

The first time Larson went to Gatto's classroom she was immediately impressed by the energy Gatto put into her teaching. The physical organization was consistent with a practice theory of literacy learning in that the room itself facilitated dynamic interaction and texts had authentic purposes. She did not have the ubiquitous teacher's desk that tells students the teacher is the authority. She had her own desk in the rectangle she made of student desks. Clearly Gatto was in charge though. She bellowed out instructions, charging her student to learn. Some might think she was hard on the students, but the activities and learning the children were doing were grounded in authentic interactions and a profound respect for persons.

Gatto used the physical space to provide the children with a common environment and common experiences for them to think about in relation to their own lives. In this classroom, however, learning traveled. The classroom was not the only physical space for learning. Field trips enabled students to learn across time and space, and to connect their school experiences to life experiences beyond school. In this way, Gatto breached the traditional boundaries between home and school, or in and out of school, in meaningful ways (Larson, 2005).

For example, one day when Larson arrived, students were building raised planters for the nursing home at which they volunteer each month as part of a building unit based on simple machines. The nursing home visits were part of a community service activity that lasted over several years. Gatto brought in big pieces of timber and the hardware needed to construct the planters that students had designed to make it easier for the senior citizens who use wheelchairs to garden. She and her husband had precut the materials that weekend. The day before students had worked on inclines in their unit on simple machines. During one observation of a group of students working on their planter, two boys spontaneously made connections to the concept of incline. One child, while setting a large leg post onto the crossbeam, said, 'Hey, an incline,' smiling to his partner. The partner looked back and said, 'Yeah, cool,' and smiled back. Students were working on a project for a real audience and with a real purpose (for nursing home residents to use in planting) and were able to spontaneously connect the building activity to science content.

THE CURRICULUM

In the present skills-only curriculum environment, it is increasingly difficult for teachers to design and implement their own curriculum. However, Gatto is undaunted in her commitment to teach what she knows is culturally relevant and meaningful to her students (Ball, 1995; Ladson-Billings, 1994; Lee, 2001). She continues to implement her own curriculum, taking careful account of local, state and national standards, in spite of outside pressures. Through a careful balance of defiance and conformity, Gatto carves out her own space, a tactical space (de Certeau, 1984), within which meaningful learning occurs (Larson and Gatto, 2004).

Gatto builds on the concept of curriculum as inquiry (Dewey, 1938; Gallas, 1994; Liem, 1981; Short et al., 1996; Wells, 1999; 2000) in constructing a classroom where students participate in authentic activities. We define authentic activities as those in which an answer or goal is not predetermined, one in which the audience and purpose of the activities are real (cf. Edelsky, 1991; Nystrand, 1997) and co-constructed by both teacher and students. Classroom activities are multifaceted and multilayered so that a range of complex, goal-directed learning activities (Cole, 1996; Rogoff, 2003) occur simultaneously, which themselves inform decisions about curricula, the physical environment and the nature of social interaction. Activity goals are initially decided by the teacher, and then laminated with children's goals as the learning progresses.

TRUSTING RELATIONSHIPS

A key part of understanding what NLS looks like in Gatto's classroom is to unpack the nature of the social relations among classroom community members. Gatto believes in the primacy of social relationships when planning and implementing her curriculum. She constructs a classroom social structure that centers on the concept of 'team'. Team-building is an explicit goal of Gatto's overall curriculum and her field trips in particular. Gatto plans team-building activities from the beginning of school. For example, during the first week of school the class always spends a night on an overnight retreat that provides key opportunities for students to learn to care for one another. Gatto might surprise them with a midnight hike on camping trips, for example, where only she has a flashlight. As a consequence, students need to rely on each other in order to navigate the trails safely. Interaction in the classroom tends to be much more relaxed and conversational after the first overnight each year. The first month of school is spent constructing routines and rituals for equipment and materials use so all team members are responsible and feel ownership for the entire classroom environment and for the nature of their interactions. In a unique activity, the children analyze videotapes of themselves working together to better understand how interaction builds relationships and commitment to learning together.

The team concept facilitates students taking responsibility for their own learning and for assuming leadership roles in various activities. The children negotiate rules, discipline procedures and instructional routines in ways that move beyond offering students 'choice'. Offering choice is often implemented as a simplistic form of a 'student-centered' curriculum that is rooted in behaviorism. It tends to be used to write classroom rules that end up looking an awful lot like what the teacher wanted in the first place. Simply offering children choice is not necessarily sufficient to transform social and power relations. However, by shifting responsibility for learning to the team, Gatto does more that 'give' choice, she asks students to take responsibility for co-constructing their own learning and the learning of their classmates and teacher.

In Gatto's classroom, interaction is conversational rather than didactic (Gutierrez, 1993; Nystrand, 1997) and follows students' ideas and topics (Gallas, 1994; Liem, 1981; Rogoff, 1996; Wells, 1999). Gatto relinquishes power as knowledge-holder by encouraging a dialogic script (Nystrand, 1997) among classroom community members (see Chapter 1 for a discussion of classroom discourse patterns and their consequences). Gatto's use of dialogic script supports the co-construction of knowledge and affords space for student-initiated ideas for learning activities, questions for investigation and problems to solve.

CURRICULUM UNITS

Curriculum activities are centered on a thematic unit that lasts three to four months. Gatto selects the themes based on national standards in all content areas (for example, National Council of Teachers of English Standards for English Language Arts) and her determination about how best to meet the content requirements of her district while maintaining her commitment to construct authentic, theoretically sound literacy learning events.

The use of thematic units, supported by extensive field trips and culminating projects, enables her students to understand how actions, knowledge, language and materials in the world are interrelated (Larson, 2005). Although Gatto initially selects the topics, the units scaffold, or assist, complex interactions between students, students and teacher, and students and the community that, in turn, generate student questions which feed further curriculum development.

Complimentary to thematic curricular engagements, the curriculum activities are based on four key areas: Math Minds, Investigations Time, Writer's Workshop and Reading Club, all of which are woven together in a science-based curriculum frame. A description of the daily schedule may help visualize her curriculum. Each year the daily schedule is different depending on the grade and needs of kids and scheduling requirements. The following is an example from second grade:

1. Make A Word: *Using words from the unit vocabulary.*

2. Reading Club: *Read aloud from various texts that relate to the theme, then Silent Sustained Reading as Gatto meets with either individuals or small groups. The small groups use either the read aloud text or multiple readers based on the theme.*

3. Unit of study activity: *Science or social studies hands-on activity & often the read aloud or an activity from a previous small group activity leads into this.*

4. Math Minds: *Problem solving relates to theme in some way, facts work uses objects from the theme.*

5. Lunch, Recess & Special Subject: *Art, music & gym.*

6. Writer's Workshop: *Three days a week it is based on a writing-process model; the other two days a week it is a directed writing activity relating to the unit of study.*

7. Centers: *Children are free to choose from centers relating to the theme.*

Gatto uses the lengthy unit plan idea to teach authentic literacy practices in ways that do not just reify (for example, reduce to commodities to be taught) literacies 'outside' school.

The Urban Botanist's Project conducted in a local park is an example of Gatto's units. The unit began with students reading biographies of three botanists: George Washington Carver, the famous African-American botanist,

Alice Eastwood, the first woman botanist, and Carl Linneaus, the developer of the classification system for plants. The children selected a biography of their own choosing to read. Biography groups discussed the aspects of their books that were interesting and determined the elements of the biography genre. Finally, they wrote their own biographies. As a scaffold for students' biographies, the children thought about and discussed what biographers think about when they write while Gatto read aloud. The children listed the kinds of information biographers must need (birthdate, place of birth, where did s/he live, what did s/he do, who were the parents, where did s/he die, how did s/he die, what was the person's race, did the person have kids?).

The project itself involved extended research in Rochester's Ellison Park each month so they could observe the trees and document how they changed over the course of the seasons. Each student adopted a tree that was visited monthly to document observations of tree characteristics, its interactions with the environment and its changes. Each child had a journal where they recorded questions and predictions (a professional literacy), described each park trip from their point of view, took notes using field guides for identification, logged measurements, illustrated with labels and drew maps.

The class produced a guide of the trees and plants using digital pictures of the trees and activities they conducted. Small groups worked on various parts of the guide. The children used Gatto's direction for what to look for or do, but then their questions became the impetus for further interactions and investigations. They placed the digital photographs and descriptions of the common plants found in the park in an information kiosk for visitors that included a botany map of the park with their trees marked off and information about them posted. They produced flyers that visitors could take with them and a teacher's manual. The students realized there were many schools within walking distance of the park and that teachers rarely went. They hoped the manual would promote more field trips to the area. The guide is filled with the children's descriptions of the activities they completed in the park, with a few additional ideas of their own. The unit is full of authentic literacy practices that build on both school-based learning and on multimodal literacies needed for participation in contemporary society.

The literacy practices constructed and used in this classroom are authentically related to practices in everyday life, including both Gatto's practices and the practices her students bring from home. The physical environment reflects these practices. Students observe and care for animals and organize and use materials in authentic ways. The classroom is not a stage where children rehearse for real life. Through extensive use of field trips the students gain access to the social and cultural practices of 'real' life to which they may not otherwise have access. We will focus on Gatto's field trip practices in more detail in the following section.

■ KEY FEATURES OF PRACTICE

Gatto's design and use of field trips is one example of how the curriculum, physical environment and social interaction come together in meaningful literacy learning activities. Gatto uses field trips as key curriculum components that teach students the literacies required for participation in school, for participation in life outside of school and to build social relationships across time and space. Field trips fall into three categories: overnight trips, day trips and 'regular' trips typically taken in this district (see Table 2.2).

Table 2.2 Sample of field trips over three years[2]

Overnight trips	Day trips	Typical district trips
■ Camping	■ Nursing home	■ Art gallery
■ Zoo	– 24 visits	■ Children's museum
■ Boston (Ocean Life)	■ Local arts high school	■ Museum of science
– Farmer's museum	■ Local college	■ Local country museum
– Children's museum	■ Niagara Falls	■ Neighborhood library
– Aquarium	– Aquarium	■ Neighborhood bank
– Seafood restaurant	– Vivarium	
– Beach study	– The falls	
■ Kentucky	■ Ice skating	
– Videoconferences	■ Local park (scientific exploration)	
– Funeral home		
– Partner classrooms	– 12 trips for water quality study and botany study	
– Family homes		
– Slumber party		
– Western Kentucky University		
– Nature reserve sleepover		

All field trips are curriculum based, provide authentic experiences beyond the students' everyday lives and are explicitly focused on community building across contexts (for example, in and out of school). The curriculum facilitates students learning the literacy practices of communities, both professional and everyday, through participation in complex thematic unit studies and their related field trips.[3]

Gatto explicitly states that field trips are not play time, however, students perceive field trips as one of the activities that make this classroom 'fun' (Larson and Gatto, 2004). Carl explained it this way when talking about the upcoming three-day field trip to the Boston seacoast as part of their ocean unit:

> *She teach like a fun projects and we're going to learn science by Boston we're gonna go to the aquarium and we're gonna have a little fun. Like we're gonna have a pool party and we're gonna go to McDonald's. But I think the best part is learning in the aquarium*

Students connect content learning to field trips although they sometimes do not see content traditionally. Jackie wrote in her Boston field trip journal that, 'Everything that I saw at the Farmer's Museum was that you can learn history in a fun kind of way to look and to have fun with history cause it could be fun'.

Building on students' experiences in museums, they decided to turn a butterfly project into a museum complete with guided tours. Students analyzed literacy practices in museums and used these practices in the butterfly museum project. They produced signs, invitations, guided 'scripts' and tour schedules. They invited the whole school, parents and community members. The opening event was documented on the local evening news.

ANALYSIS OF A SERIES OF LESSONS ON A THEME

Each year, Gatto takes her students on an extended trip that brings together all thematic study into a culminating experience. One class trip to Kentucky provides a case example of the role of field trips in this classroom.[4] This trip was a richly engaging long-distance event that took intensive co-ordination and fund-raising on the part of two teachers and their students over time and space using email and videoconferences, for example. Called 'scientific summits', videoconferences or 'cyber trips' (Larson, 2005) were grounded in academic and scientific language and literacy practices. Students presented their research to each other using the literacies, discourses and practices of scientists. Gatto prepared them for air travel (Figure 2.1) in the new high security context in the USA by taking them to the airport to go through security, giving them access to the cultural capital associated with air travel (Nespor, 2000).

Figure 2.1 Digital video still: on the plane

This trip enacted the three principles Gatto uses to guide her fields trips by bringing together all the units the class studied throughout the year in the curriculum principle. The content of the units was reunited as students experienced ideas and practices they has studied throughout the year. The second principle of engaging in authentic sociocultural practices beyond the students' lives was enacted as students built relationships across time and space with their new friends in Kentucky using multimodal textual practices (videoconferences, emails, cards and letters). To develop these relationships, students participated in the videoconferences already mentioned, traveled by air to a southern rural community and attended demonstrations in university classrooms (Figure 2.2). The curriculum principle connects to the authenticity principle in the scientific activities in which children engaged.

Figure 2.2 Digital video still: university demonstration

The community-building principle was evident in the prolonged interaction between Gatto's students and the Kentucky students during the trip. The slumber party (Figure 2.3), an overnight at the nature center and spending the night at local family homes, all served to build a sense of a team on an adventure. Children grew closer over the course of the trip. Gatto's students shared a common meaningful experience they will remember for a long time and developed friendships with new community members that were constructed over time and in both cyberspace and physical space.

Figure 2.3 Digital video still: slumber party in Kentucky

Gatto provided experiences which extended students' everyday lives by moving beyond 'exposure' to genuine participation in experiences that gave students access to literacy practices, cultural capital and discourses of power commonly denied them in more traditional classrooms (Larson, 2005). Gatto explicitly uses field trips in her curriculum as one tool for students to participate in literacies needed for participation in an information economy. For example, the cyber 'scientific summits' afforded students an opportunity to participate in authentic scientific discourse using communicative practices common in academic and corporate contexts, giving students access to discourses of power that traditionally defined field trips or the textbook-based science curriculum do not (Larson, 2005).

We turn now to our interview with Brian Street, renowned scholar and key figure in NLS research. Street has visited Gatto's classroom and thus can give personal as well as scholarly insight into her classroom.

INTERVIEW WITH BRIAN STREET

WHAT ASPECTS OF THIS CASE STUDY DO YOU FEEL REFLECT THE MAIN TENETS OF NLS?

From both my reading of this chapter and my experience in Gatto's classroom, I am struck by the use of *multiple literacy practices* across community/classroom/new environments, each with their own literacy practices. This chapter documents how Gatto has made use of NLS as she and her students construct and use multiple literacies across contexts. In this context, these practices can be described in terms of genres and modes. I am defining genre as a type of formal and informal text such as notes, letters and academic papers. All of these genres (and more) are used instructionally in classrooms. A mode is a regularized, organized set of resources for meaning-making such as image, gaze (teacher and student), movement, music, speech and writing, among others. What I am interested in understanding from an NLS perspective is how genres and modes vary across disciplines, subjects and fields. Teachers also switch between genres within a single class event: the teacher and students use switching to negotiate between different literacies, although frequently they fail to reflect on them or to mark their presence, leaving some children lost as to where they are (cf. Street et al., forthcoming). Gatto's class is a wonderful example of a teacher who is aware of what is involved in such switching.

For example, the teacher and students in her class used a variety of visual modes to discuss and present ideas such as notes, overheads (for example, note-taking, brainstorming and formal presentations), chalkboard-writing, sign-out sheets and observational notes for science projects. Children discussed biography in groups, listed information and then wrote accounts whilst Gatto read aloud. Her instructional practices helped to mark these genre boundaries and scaffold children's understanding of them. At the same time, the switching was fluid and constructed socially over time. Gatto, then, assisted her students in 'taking hold' of literacy by exposing them to variety and difference in meaning-making practices and guiding their own possession of specific literacy practices.

▨ WHAT DO YOU SEE AS THE MOST IMPORTANT CONTRIBUTION NLS CAN MAKE TO CLASSROOM PRACTICE?

New Literacy Studies can offer a solid framework for building upon what pupils bring with them from home and community and we see this in Gatto's classroom. As Hull and Schultz (2002) argue, the major contribution to understanding schooled literacy in the past decade has been studies of out-of-school practice. What Gatto does here is very like what researchers and teachers have tried to do in *Literacies across Educational Contexts* (Street, 2005) reporting on their similar experiences bridging home and school. These researchers extend students' literacy repertoires via new experiences, thereby moving NLS beyond just romanticizing 'the local' at the expense of not giving pupils the 'literacies of power' (cf. Delpit; Brandt). Gatto helps pupils reflect on their home accomplishments, extend them and learn new literacies through innovative approaches such as the use of field trips to places like Kentucky. An NLS framework helps us to understand how Gatto and her students reflect critically on uses and meanings of literacy, and use the class as a platform for reflection not just for delivery.

▨ WHAT IDEAS DO YOU HAVE TO HELP TEACHERS UNDERSTAND THE FOUNDATIONS OF NLS?

I use NLS to help teachers and researchers understand the importance of reflecting on our own assumptions and problematizing what we might otherwise take for granted (for example, dominant views of the great divide regarding the role of literacy in society). Understanding literacy as ideological can help teachers unpack their assumptions regarding schooled literacy versus other literacies, and regarding pedagogy and how people learn literacies. In other words, to understand the use and meaning of schooled literacy, those interested in ethnographic approaches have to not just reject it but redefine it. To do this, teachers need to describe their own practices and put into perspective what schooling cherishes in terms of literacy and why. The purpose is to relate our own practices to (a) children's out-of-school literacies and (b) classroom literacies and the role of pedagogy and learning.

▨ WHAT ARE THE IMPLICATIONS OF NLS FOR LITERACY RESEARCH IN THE CONTEMPORARY CONTEXT?

New Literacy Studies addresses the need to re-frame theory and methodology through the use of an ethnographic perspective to view variation in the communicative practices required in contemporary society. This does require a break with the dominant tendency at present to emphasize 'skills-based', centralized, packaged and scripted programmes, and instead to research examples of ways in which teachers build upon the actual uses and meanings of literacy our pupils engage with and on their meaning-making and creative potential.

CONCLUSION

We have shown that in a classroom based on NLS principles, students do not understand literacy learning to be restricted to any one place or time but, rather, that it occurs in everyday activities in multiple contexts and at different times. The variation in learning spaces Gatto's students experienced provided rich opportunities for full participation in both everyday community activities and school-based learning events. As a result, the division between 'inside' and 'outside' is blurred as learning occurs across time and space (Leander, 2001). In addition, students develop an expanded understanding of what it means to learn literacy across local and more global contexts as they move between cultures and communities (Luke, 2003).

New Literacy Studies emphasizes literacy as a more complex social practice than traditional pedagogy, curricula and assessments address. As Street (1997; 1999; 2005) has argued, curricula and assessment that reduce literacy to simple, mechanistic skills fail to recognize, or use meaningfully, the richly complex literacy practices of teachers and students in everyday life. In order for students to learn and contribute to the richness and complexity of literacy practices in contemporary society, we need literacy curricula and assessment that reflect that richness and complexity. New Literacy Studies offers a rich lens within which to develop, implement and research just such practices.

In this chapter, we discussed the roots of NLS and presented a set of propositions that form the foundation of this theoretical framework. We grounded the theory in a case study of veteran urban teacher Lynn Gatto, and Brian Street then offered his insight into Gatto's practice based on his research and his visit to her classroom. In the following chapter, we present critical literacy as the next theoretical framework examined.

NOTES

1 See Hull and Schultz (2002), Lankshear and Knobel (2003a) and Street (forthcoming) for discussion of the history of NLS.

2 The following section is adapted from Larson (2005).

3 Only the nursing-home trips are not based on one of Gatto's thematic units. The goal for nursing-home trips focuses on community membership in general and on helping students understand how they can serve the community through service to others in particular. Through sustained interaction with residents and staff, students gain experiential knowledge of the discourses of aging and community service.

4 Table 2.2 gives examples of extended trips over three years.

CHAPTER 3

Critical Literacy

In this chapter, we provide an overview of the concept of critical literacy and outline how it can inform classroom practice. This is no simple task, because there is no singular, normative version of critical literacy. Rather, it is a concept that has been shaped by various theoretical paradigms over the years and formulated in practice in ways that are deeply contextualized and specifically situated. This means that providing a historical overview of its development is well nigh impossible. Nevertheless, we will, in this introductory section, trace critical literacy's origins in critical theory and pedagogy, and offer a brief review of other theoretical influences on its development.

HISTORICAL GROUND

The concept of critical literacy, although rooted in the tenets of critical theory propounded by the Frankfurt school at the beginning of the twentieth century, came to the fore with the work of Paulo Freire mid-century. In 1946, Freire became the Director of the Pernambuco Department of Education and Culture in Brazil, where he developed educational programs for adult workers. Freire formulated a successful literacy campaign in the early 1960s in which hundreds of sugarcane workers took part in a literacy program that incorporated critical pedagogy. Based on critical social theory, critical pedagogy locates schooling in political context and constantly challenges teachers and researchers to uncover implicit oppressions (such as inequities based on 'race', class, gender, sexual orientation and other aspects of identity). Freire explains that his program was rooted in a model that fostered student creativity as well as empowerment:

From the beginning, we rejected ... a purely mechanistic literacy program and considered the problem of teaching adults how to read in relation to the awakening of their consciousness ... We wanted a literacy program which would be an introduction to the democratization of culture, a program with human beings as its subjects rather than as patient recipients, a program which itself would be an act of creation, capable of releasing other creative acts, one in which students would develop the impatience and vivacity which characterize search and invention. (Freire, 1972: 43)

This model was to be extended throughout Brazil until the military coup of 1964 precipitated Freire's exile from Brazil and the extension of his work to other countries in South America, in particular, Cuba.

Freire's pedagogy was based on a number of key concepts. First, literacy education should be concerned with raising the *conscientização*, or critical consciousness, of learners. Perhaps one of the most well known of Freire's tenets is that, 'Reading does not consist merely of decoding the written word of language; rather, it is preceded by and intertwined with knowledge of the world' (Freire and Macedo, 1987: 29), commonly described as reading the word and the world. Literacy, therefore, is primarily concerned with the relationship between ideology and political consciousness. Second, Freire propounded that dialogue was at the heart of learning and that teachers and students should participate in dialogic discourse if meaningful learning was to occur (Shor and Freire, 1987b). In this model, students and teachers are partners in the learning process, rather than participating in hierarchical models of power. Third, Freire argued that teaching should recognize students' prior knowledge and exhorted educators to avoid 'banking' models of education, 'a process of teaching in which the teacher fills the supposedly empty heads of learners with his or her words' (Freire and Macedo, 1987: 34).

Although Freire's work has been central to the development of critical literacy, there has been critique of his model of literacy. For example, Street suggested that Freire's conception of literacy was based on assumptions about the link between cognition and literacy and that Freire's model had 'not entirely shrugged off the assumptions of the "autonomous" model' (Street, 1984: 14). In addition, there were questions relating to the notion of empowerment, given that it is rooted in modernist assumptions about power and the ability of educators to 'liberate' a particular group of learners. Challenging the assumption that empowerment is unidirectional is a key criticism of critical pedagogy, a concept that was related to the work of critical educators such as Freire and developed by theorists who drew from

Marxism and the Frankfurt school in their critique of normative schooling, for example, Giroux (1988) and Shor (1992; 1996).[1]

Critical literacy enjoyed prominence in a number of countries in which it was related to issues of struggle and liberation. In particular, it has a long tradition in South American countries, such as Nicaragua and Cuba, and has also been a key concern of South African educators who linked it to the struggle against apartheid (Janks, 2000). However, the development of critical literacy within the school system, rather than adult educational programs, has been most marked in Australia.

IMPLICATIONS FOR CLASSROOMS

Peter Freebody's and Allan Luke's work in the field of critical literacy has been highly influential in informing classroom practice (Freebody and Luke, 2003; Luke and Freebody, 1997a; 1999). In 1990, they proposed a four-resource model for reading which has been widely cited and adapted in various ways in educational sites (Freebody and Luke, 1990). In this model, they proposed that there were four key roles for the reader: as code breaker (relating to decoding/encoding competence); meaning maker (focusing on reader response); text user (pragmatic competence) and text critic (critical response). However, revisiting this model in the late 1990s, Freebody and Luke were keen to point out that their original model, like all normative models, was historically situated and needed to be revised to take into account the developments in theoretical and empirical understandings of literacy.

In their revised model, they suggested that the following principles related to practices rather than reader roles, the latter concept being more appropriate to psychological, individualized formulations of reading. They suggested that critical readers and writers needed to:

- *Break the code of texts*: recognizing and using the fundamental features and architecture of written texts, including alphabet, sounds in words, spelling, conventions and patterns of sentence structure and text.

- *Participate in the meanings of text*: understanding and composing meaningful written, visual and spoken texts from within the meaning systems of particular cultures, institutions, families, communities, nation-states and so forth.

- *Use texts functionally*: traversing the social relations around texts; knowing about and acting on the different cultural and social functions that various texts perform both inside and outside school and knowing that these functions shape the way texts are structured, their tone, their degree of formality and their sequence of components.

- *Critically analyze and transform texts*: understanding and acting on the knowledge that texts are not neutral, that they represent particular views and silence other points of view, influence people's ideas; and that their designs and discourses can be critiqued and redesigned, in novel and hybrid ways. (Luke and Freebody, 1999:np).

This model has not been without critique. For example, Lankshear and Knobel (2004a) suggest that it is inappropriate for textual practices that are rooted in contemporary, multimodal communicative practices. They argue that in textual practices related to new technologies, the roles of text participant and text user are often indistinguishable and that Freebody and Luke's model is primarily aimed at a normative concept of schooled literacy practices rather than the complex, everyday practices of the digitized world. However, we would argue Lankshear and Knobel's (2004a) alternative analysis of roles related to literacy practices embedded in digital technologies (text designer; text bricoleur; text mediator and text jammer, discussed at length in Chapter 4 of this book), emphasizes text production rather than text analysis and, whilst in many activities these practices are indistinguishable, in some they are not. However, the models offered by Freebody and Luke (2003) and Lankshear and Knobel (2004a) both speak to the complexities of contemporary practices in which children and young people are text producers *and* analysts in both schooled and out-of-school contexts. The challenge is to embed these models effectively into teacher education in order to ensure that critical literacy as a theoretical tool can be translated into practice.

Given the range and diversity of various models of critical literacy, work that has striven to identify key underlying concepts has been valuable in drawing out some of the consequences of the different models. For example, Janks (2000) suggests that diverse models of critical literacy are conceptually different in relation to their emphasis on one of four aspects: domination, access, diversity and design. Domination models operate on the assumption that language and other symbolic forms reproduce social inequalities and that critical language awareness (CLA) can enable the deconstruction of power within texts. Access issues are also central because of questions about how learners can access dominant models without sacrificing their own literacy practices and histories. Of course, this was a question that haunted genre theorists for many years (Cope and Kalantzis, 1993) and is central to issues of critical pedagogy. Janks points out that diversity, whilst providing opportunities for productive power, is often beset with the consequences of relations of dominance. The fourth aspect she emphasizes, design, recognizes the importance of production for transformation and reconstruction. Janks suggests that these four aspects, domination, access, diversity and design, are interdependent:

> Any one of domination, diversity, access or design without the others creates a problematic imbalance. Genre theory without creativity runs the risk of reifying existing genres; deconstruction without reconstruction or design reduces human agency; diversity without access ghettoizes students. Domination without difference and diversity loses the ruptures that produce contestation and change. (2000: 178–9)

Critical literacy has also been influenced by work in the fields of feminism, racism and queer theory. There has been extensive work on ways in which normative models of literacy serve to position women in subjugated roles (Brady and Hernández, 1993; Rockhill, 1993). In addition, post-structuralist feminist theorists have provided a thorough critique of critical pedagogy that, they claim, has often positioned learners rather passively in relation to the supposedly more knowledgeable and 'liberating' teachers (Gore, 1992; 1993; Luke and Gore, 1992). This seam of work has informed more recent deliberations on the nature of critical literacy and the need to ensure that the critical knowledge and skills learners bring to the site of learning are recognized (Alvermann et al., 1999).

In addition to post-structuralist feminism, literacy theory rooted in antiracist and multicultural traditions is important to the critical literacy paradigm. For example, the work of Shuaib Meacham in the USA has illuminated fundamental issues in relation to the literacy practices of African-Americans. He has demonstrated how textual practices rooted in slavery are embedded in hip hop as a cultural form and illustrates how many rap lyrics provide a strong critical counter to hegemonic constructions of power in a racist society (Meacham, 2003). Other theoretical traditions that focus on specific aspects of life on the margins also inform critical literacy theory. Queer theorists suggest that heteronormative models permeate constructions of the literacy curriculum and ensure that literacy practices reflecting queer concerns are marginalized and 'othered'

(Vicars, forthcoming). Some of the theorists referred to above would not necessarily locate their work within the critical literacy paradigm, yet it is clear their work is both informed by critical literacy theory and, in turn, shapes the discourse in important ways.

Given the complex nature of critical literacy and the varied theoretical influences on it, we would not want to provide a single definition. The various models outlined in this chapter are all underpinned by the principle that critical literacy is 'learning to read and write as part of the processes of becoming conscious of one's experience as historically constructed within specific power relations. The goal of critical literacy ... is to challenge these unequal power relations' (Anderson and Irvine, 1993: 82). However, from the work reviewed so far, other tenets also emerge as particularly important to a critical approach to literacy education. These are summarized in Table 3.1.

Table 3.1 Key tenets of critical literacy

1. Literacy is not a neutral technology, it is always ideologically situated. It is shaped by power and, in turns, shapes subjects and discourses (Freebody and Luke, 1990).

2. Learners are differently positioned in relation to access to dominant literacy discourses through aspects such as 'race', class, culture, gender, language, sexual orientation and physical abilities (Meacham, 2003; Vicars, forthcoming).

3. Critical literacy practices can foster political awareness and social change (Freebody and Luke, 1990; Freire and Macedo, 1987).

4. Critical literacy involves any or all of the following: having a critical perspective on language and literacy itself, on particular texts and/or on wider social practices (Lankshear et al., 1997).

5. Learners' own cultural and semiotic resources should be utilized within classrooms and their critical stances towards these resources recognized and extended (Comber, 2001a; Comber and Simpson, 2001; Dyson, 2001a; 2002; Vasquez, 2001; 2004a; 2004b).

6. Text design and production can provide opportunities for critique and potential transformation of discourses of power (Janks, 2000; Vasquez, 2001; 2004a; 2004b).

Although the field of critical literacy is extensive and there are many examples of practice that draw from its theoretical framework, there are relatively few accounts of critical literacy in primary classrooms. Comber (2003) has argued that work undertaken since the 1980s which critiqued normalizing discourses in early childhood has shifted the ground for critical literacy theorists and teachers, and there have been subsequent developments in relation to the application of key tenets of critical literacy in primary schools. We present some of this work below as examples of research that have explored aspects of critical literacy in early childhood.

IMPLICATIONS FOR RESEARCHING LITERACY

Anne Haas Dyson's research has illuminated, in fine detail, how young children recontextualize the stuff of home and community in school settings (Dyson, 1997; 1999; 2001b; 2002). Recontextualization involves transforming and reshaping cultural material across semiotic modes and social practices and, in Dyson's studies, it is clear that the children experienced discursive shifts as they transferred material across boundaries. As Dyson suggests: 'when children translated cultural material … across the boundaries of different practices involving different semiotic technologies, they could be stopped short, as the textual and conceptual knowledge embedded in their everyday and playful practices was disrupted and brought into reflective awareness' (2002: 93).

The children encounter semiotic, social and ideological tensions as they move material from one context to another. In Dyson's studies, questions of 'raced', classed and gendered identities permeated children's social engagement in classroom literacy practices and this work raised ideological tensions and reflections. This enabled skillful teachers to draw out important concepts such as racism and sexism for careful deliberation by these children in elementary grades. As Comber notes, 'While [Dyson] doesn't name her work as part of a critical literacy tradition, the questions she explores are at the heart of a social justice project in early literacy education' (Comber, 2003: 359).

Barbara Comber's own work has been highly influential in raising awareness of critical literacy in early childhood and primary traditions (Comber, 2003). From her extensive research across a range of contexts, she has suggested that critical literacy involves a number of key principles and repertoires for practice:

- engaging with local realities;
- researching and analyzing language–power relationships, practices and effects;
- mobilizing students' knowledge and practices;

- (re) designing texts with political and social intent and real-world use;

- subverting taken-for-granted 'school' texts;

- focusing on students' use of local cultural texts, and

- examining how power is exercised and by whom. (Comber, 2003: 276)

Comber has conducted research within classrooms that has involved children becoming engaged in environmental issues within their own neighborhood (Comber et al., 2001b) and emphasizes the localized nature of much critical literacy practice. However, critical literacy can involve analysis of globalized narratives as well as local ones and, indeed, explore notions of 'glocalization' (Kraidy, 1999) as they play out in local contexts. Important in this work is the emphasis on children as critical agents who bring to the classroom a wealth of critical insights on their world and who do not need to acquire a set of print-based literacy skills and knowledge before they can engage in critical literacy practices.

In the following case study, we draw on the experiences of Vivian Vasquez to illuminate how the key tenets of critical literacy can be integrated into the curriculum and pedagogy of a primary classroom. Although Vasquez has now moved into higher education, she spent many years as an elementary teacher in Canada and has documented some of the innovative and exciting work she developed there in a number of publications (Vasquez, 2001; 2004a; 2004b). In this chapter, we outline aspects of Vasquez's work undertaken in a pre-school centre in Canada.

CLASSROOM CASE STUDY: VIVIAN VASQUEZ, ONTARIO, CANADA

Vasquez, in a teaching career that spanned 14 years before she moved into teacher education at American University in Washington, taught children aged between 3 and 9 at various stages of her career. While teaching in an elementary school in Canada, prior to becoming involved in teacher education, Vasquez represented the pre-school to third grade teachers in the role of division chair for many years. In this capacity, she attempted to provide opportunities for colleagues to participate in discussions on various aspects of teaching and learning, and informal professional development events that took place on a voluntary basis after school hours. During this period, she also undertook a number of specialist qualifications in primary education, special education and reading.

As with the other teachers whose work is featured in this book, Vasquez also undertook a masters qualification. She studied for hers at Mount Saint Vincent University in Nova Scotia, Canada. This course offered participants the opportunity to undertake courses in other countries, such as Australia and England. Vasquez attended a course in Australia, at which time she met Barbara Comber and her colleagues, who were active in critical literacy research. Meeting Comber was a turning point in her career, as Vasquez became excited about the prospect of introducing these approaches in her Canadian classroom and, on her return, began to develop a range of critical literacy projects. She began writing and presenting locally, nationally and internationally. Eventually, Vasquez undertook doctoral studies at Indiana University, Bloomington, where she completed a dissertation on negotiating critical literacies with young children while working with Jerome C. Harste, who at the time had also been exploring possibilities for critical literacy in school settings.

Vasquez is currently an assistant professor at American University in Washington, DC. She continues to work on critical literacy projects with local kindergarten and elementary teachers in Virginia. She also ensures that a critical approach is taken to literacy practices in the university sessions she teaches. In the following section, we outline the approaches Vasquez took to critical literacy in her elementary classes. The description of the classroom that follows is presented differently than the other classroom case examples in this book. Because neither of us conducted research in Vasquez's classroom, we asked her to describe her practice herself. It is, therefore, her words we use here and we have adapted the format slightly, which involved changing the account to third person in places, in order to achieve consistency with the case studies presented in other chapters.

CONTEXT

The school which features in this case study is located in a very diverse, multi-ethnic, middle-class community just outside Metropolitan Toronto in Ontario, Canada. Although the socioeconomic context has been designated 'middle-class', this was not straightforward. Within this area, there were homes occupied by more than one family. The classroom described in this account has featured in Vasquez's illuminating account of her critical literacy approach, *Negotiating Critical Literacies with Young Children* (Vasquez, 2004b). It was a half-day pre-school class that met from 8.45 a.m. to 11.15 a.m.

PHYSICAL ENVIRONMENT AND RESOURCES

Because the curriculum was constantly being renewed and developed as a result of Vasquez's commitment to a critical literacy approach, Vasquez had to ensure that the physical space of the classroom was flexible enough to incorporate changes and provide room for innovation and improvisation. Vasquez collected together a wide range of rich resources such as videos, news articles, music, books, everyday texts, art posters and websites. Vasquez also identified and brought into the classroom the materials needed to support the study of the different issues that interested the class. This necessitated keen observation as a teacher, as she had to be alert to the themes that were surfacing in classroom and playground talk, reading practices and daily classroom activities, and then support them as necessary with the provision of resources. Vasquez felt that this observation was an important feature of her practice, as it enabled her to build on children's interests in important and reflective ways.

The classroom was organized into different areas, such as an open area for class meetings, an art area and a library. Vasquez's aim was to offer an environment that promoted children's autonomy and provided them with a rich range of multimedia resources to inform their work. The classroom provided spaces for small-group and large-group work, and chairs and a sofa were scattered around the room. Vasquez felt that it was important that children could access the resources they needed when they wanted, and organize themselves in ways that met their needs at the time, so that she could work intensively with children. Vasquez did not have a teacher's desk, but spent her time circulating the classroom, working with individuals and groups. She states:

> I suppose one way to describe my classroom would be to say that it was not typical of pre-school or kindergarten classrooms. For instance I didn't have a calendar set up, nor did I have posted alphabet cards or word walls. Instead, my classroom made use of a calendar like one you might have in the kitchen at home and loads of print materials pertaining to our inquiries. My students thrived in this environment, they wrote stories like any other primary school child but they also learned to create things like petitions and surveys, which were tools they used to do their social justice work.

This carefully constructed environment offered children physical, social, emotional and cognitive spaces in which to engage in their critical projects and, in this model, the teacher also had space, space to become a co-researcher and participant in collaborative activities.

THE CURRICULUM

Because of her educational philosophy, Vasquez felt that any curriculum had to emerge in an organic way from the cultural and social practices in which both students and teachers engaged:

> First let me say that I believe a critical literacy curriculum needs to be lived and that whatever form it takes should arise from the social and political conditions that unfold in communities in which we live. So it could begin locally and move to more global issues and spaces or it could begin from a global perspective as world events and topics are reflected in the sociopolitical issues that unfold in a community. Given this take on critical literacy, I don't believe it can be traditionally taught. In other words, as teachers, attempting to work through a critical literacy perspective, I believe we need to incorporate a critical stance in our everyday lives in order to find ways to help children understand and analyze the social and political issues around them.

Vasquez drew from the work of Luke and Freebody (1997a and b), Janks (2000) and Comber (2001a) in the development of a theoretical framework for her practice. She also incorporated postmodernist and feminist theory, as well as being influenced by the work of Bakhtin and Foucault. This dynamic and challenging mix spurred her on to develop ways of working that transgressed normative models. For example, she insisted that the curriculum was, in fact, negotiated between her and the students, and not imposed by external constraints:

> Working from a critical perspective, my desire was to construct spaces where social justice issues could be raised and a critical curriculum negotiated with my students. A critical literacy framework helped me to take up issues of social justice and equity with my students. Negotiation and contestation were a central part of our discussions rather than a more familiar process of discovering 'the' best way. I envisioned learning as a process of adjusting and reconstructing what we knew rather than of accumulating information. In our classroom, the focus was on using the issues from the social lives of children to construct and sustain a critical curriculum. The children and I researched our world together and produced data together in the form of an audit trail which was displayed on a bulletin board covered with artifacts of learning such as photographs, letters, book covers and transcripts of conversations. We used this audit trail as a tool for generating and circulating meaning. Posting artifacts that represented the work we were doing was a way for us to retrace our thinking. Retracing thinking involves theorizing. As my students and I began constructing the audit trail, I thought about using it as a tool for critical conversation with them. It seemed to me that making theoretical connections visible using

artifacts might enable my students to revisit, reread, analyze and re-imagine possibilities for living a critically literate life. I also imagined that the audit trail could be a tool for building curriculum.

The audit trail was a central aspect of Vasquez's pedagogy. The children and Vasquez covered the classroom wall with their trails, known to the children as the 'Learning Wall' because they knew it was central to their learning. This wall became filled with artifacts and images that were embedded in classroom discourse and learning activities. It included photographs, book covers, posters, newspaper clippings, magazine advertisements, transcripts of conversations, a stuffed toy and Internet printouts. These artifacts and images provided a means of articulating the learning journeys undertaken by the class, as they consisted of items that had been crucial to critical classroom conversations, as well as documenting resistant practices and providing an account of the way in which the children and Vasquez demonstrated agency within the community. This agency enabled children to challenge established practices and explore issues that were relevant to their lives; to take control of their own learning in this way was a powerful process that involved co-constructing a curriculum, rather than being the passive recipients of a pre-packaged one. The 'Learning Wall' offered, therefore, a way to record the co-constructed curriculum, as well as providing a means to develop it further.

During the school year, children would refer to the audit trail, discussing and reflecting on various images and artifacts. The wall eventually reflected the class's interest in a range of issues such as gender, the environment, fairness, the media and power and control. Over the course of the school year, these issues were revisited and extended. Thus the curriculum became a living, breathing embodiment of the children's (and Vasquez's) issues and concerns, rather than a construction that was beyond the control of the classroom participants. As Vasquez notes:

My experience working with teachers attempting to engage in critical literacy shows me that in many cases, social issues are treated as variables to be added to the existing curriculum. This is done rather than using the issues to build curriculum because these issues are associated with cynicism and unpleasurable work. However, critical literacy does not necessarily involve taking a negative stance, rather it means looking at an issue or topic in different ways, analyzing it and hopefully being able to suggest possibilities for change or improvement. Often issues of social justice and equity seem to be looked upon as heavy-handed issues. The conversations that we had and the actions we took, although often serious, were very pleasurable. We enjoyed our work because the topics that we dealt with were socially significant to us.

In my experience the extent to which I was able to negotiate spaces to engage in critical literacy practices was related to the extent to which I had understood possibilities for engaging in critical literacies. The understanding or conceptualization that I am referring to is not about beliefs held in my head. The conceptualization I am referring to has to do with the extent to which I was able to act on my beliefs. In essence to 'do critical literacy theory'. As my conceptualization of critical literacies changed, I was able to create different spaces for it in the curriculum, which led to further opportunities to deepen my understanding that in turn led to the creation of even more curricular spaces. The relationship between conceptualization and negotiating spaces is therefore a recursive process.

The process that Vasquez describes here is an important one in the development of any critical literacy approach. As we outlined in Chapter 1 of this book, teachers' classroom practices are the result of a complex dynamic between theory and practice, each one informing the other. Critical literacy theories impacted on Vasquez's approaches to teaching, but the effects of these approaches and the issues raised in practice also affected the theories and Vasquez's understanding of them.

Some readers may wonder how Vasquez was able to develop a negotiated curriculum within an education system that had specific requirements. She notes that:

While my students and I negotiated a critical literacy curriculum, we were not free from curricular mandates and the threat of standardized testing. Our School Board dictated specific programs to follow. As the classroom teacher, I made sure that I understood what was expected of me through the mandated curriculum in order to demonstrate to parents, colleagues and administrators that our negotiated curriculum surpassed the required curriculum. I did this as a way of creating as much space as I could to engage in the literacy work that I felt would offer my students more opportunities for contributing to social change and that would give them access to more powerful literacies (that is, literacies that could make a difference in their lives, for example, as young people, females or underrepresented minorities).

As we discuss in Chapter 6, it is possible to comply with mandated curricula and meet those narrow requirements whilst, at the same time, moving beyond them. Vasquez realizes the importance of ensuring that the children acquire the skills, knowledge and understanding that will provide them with academic capital, but is also clear that this does not need to be achieved through a narrow focus on skills. The latter approach, although ostensibly claiming to offer marginalized groups access to schooled literacy, simply narrows their options further and creates an impoverished educational diet.

█ KEY FEATURES OF PRACTICE

Vasquez developed a number of specific approaches to the task of engaging children in critical reflection. One of the strategies she used was that of a daily 'class meeting'. These were meetings in which individual and small groups of children presented a range of topics and issues for discussion. Vasquez notes that:

> My intent was to be a participant in the meeting as opposed to being the person in charge or the chair of the meeting, without implying that I was an innocent or neutral participant. One of the concerns I had regarding child-centered pedagogies is the attitude embedded in commonly heard statements such as 'I had nothing to do with it' (curriculum), or 'It was all their idea', as though the teacher's ideologies or beliefs never played a part in what came to be curriculum. The bottom line is children participate based on the discourses, the ways of being, that have been made available for them, many of these having been introduced at school.

A child volunteer chaired these meetings. Children volunteered after agreeing on the chairperson's responsibilities and a rota was developed for chairing. Vasquez found that the majority of the children wished to chair. The chairperson would chair the meetings for a period of a week, and this role enabled children to make decisions and have enhanced status in the group for a while.

Obviously, the agenda for this daily meeting was of crucial importance in enabling the children's issues and interests to be played out. Vasquez describes how the agenda was set:

> Each class meeting was based on a meeting agenda that was developed at the start of every morning by the meeting chairperson. The agenda was created after signing in for attendance and checking to see what their job responsibilities were for the day. The individual whose job it was to be chair for the meeting moved about the room asking for 'items' to be included in the meeting agenda. Items were topics, issues, questions, discoveries and inquiries that children had. These items were then listed on a poster board and propped up on a chart stand. Sometimes the children dictated their agenda items. Other times, the children took on this job for themselves either writing using conventional or approximated spelling or drawing. Once all agenda items had been recorded in some way, the meeting began. Mostly this happened during the first 15 minutes of class. Often, children met me in the schoolyard sharing the issues they were interested in raising during class meetings. Even some of the parents showed interest and spoke with me

of having had conversations with their children while getting ready for school, regarding the issues/topics that their child was thinking about proposing for the meeting agenda.

The meeting agenda thus became a plan for the day that was shared by all. Vasquez also kept detailed notes of the day in a separate binder, which could be used by substitute/supply teachers when she was away from the classroom. During the year, this daily planning changed in that, during the class meeting, children would construct a plan for the current day, but would also consult the agenda from the previous day in order to promote continuity. Vasquez had noticed that children would often try to find the previous day's agenda when setting the agenda for the day and so, building on this observation, she made it easier for them to refer to previous work. Vasquez also noticed the children referring to items and artifacts on the audit trail as they planned for the day, which indicated how they were integrating their learning in meaningful ways.

As the class meeting progressed, Vasquez would jot down reflections on the side of the agenda. One day, the children asked Vasquez what she was doing, and she responded that she was noting down her thoughts about the issues and items that were being raised. The children stated that they would like a space to note down their reflections also, and so Vasquez responded by dividing the poster board into two sections, one of which provided a space to note down the children's reflections on the proceedings. These reflections soon became the first item to be discussed, as children revisited the previous day's concerns. Again, the children were building on previous work and making connections between their different experiences, a stark contrast to a curriculum model in which children move swiftly from objective to objective, rarely having time to reflect on their work.

◼ ANALYSIS OF A SERIES OF LESSONS ON A THEME

Given the careful way in which Vasquez developed her curriculum and pedagogical approaches, it is inevitable that the learning experiences offered to and taken up by the children were rich and varied. In the following example, Vasquez describes a particular session that indicates just how rich these experiences were.[2] The incident was provoked by a 4-year-old, Anthony, who, the day after a school barbecue attended by children, parents and teachers, told the rest of the class that he was a vegetarian and had been unable to eat the beef hamburgers and hot dogs at the barbecue.

One day as the children came into the classroom, the air was filled with excitement about the school barbecue that took place the night before. They talked about whom they saw and what they ate. They talked about bringing their left over potato chips and soda to school and argued over whether this was a healthy snack. Wanting to talk more about the school barbecue, Stefanie added the topic to the agenda for our class meeting. When her name was called out, she started by saying that she was interested to know whether there were more people who ate hamburgers or more people who ate hot dogs. To do this she stated that she was 'going to do a hand-count survey'. A quiet whisper could be heard from the back of the group followed by what seemed to be agitated conversation. Anthony, one of the boys in the class, had said to some of the children sitting beside him that he didn't eat at the barbecue because he is vegetarian and therefore he could not participate in Stefanie's survey.

We had been engaged in an inquiry about rainforests at the time of the bar-becue and had talked about the need to preserve the rainforests so that animals and people that live there would have food and shelter. We had also talked about whose interests are served and who profits and benefits from materials harvested from rainforests. For example, we discussed how multi-national companies like McDonald's, in the past, contributed to destroying rainforests by hiring suppliers who rear beef cattle on ex-rainforest land in South and Central America, thereby preventing its regeneration.

The children were upset that no one had thought about having food for veg-etarians at the barbecue and that no one had asked if there were vegetarians in our school community. The issue became a topic of concern at a number of class meetings. During one conversation, Stefanie asked, 'Who decided that we would only have beef hamburgers and hot dogs at the barbecue?' I explained that there was a committee, a group of parents and teachers that organized the barbecue and the chair of the committee was the assistant to the principal. Apparently, Stefanie had talked about the vegetarian issue with her family and her mom had encouraged her to investigate further. In conversation with some of the other children, it was revealed that many of them had also talked about this issue with their families.

Led by Stefanie, the group decided to act on their concern and problematize the marginalization of vegetarians at 'our' annual school barbecue. We started by reading the announcement flyer that the children took home advertising the School Barbecue. 'Join us for our Annual School Barbecue' was the first line of text. 'The invitation says our but doesn't really mean Anthony so it's yours and mine (pointing to other children who are not vege-tarian and herself) but not his (pointing to Anthony) and that's not fair', Melanie commented. We had done some analysis of the words used in magazine ads and how pronouns work to position readers in particular ways. Here, Melanie was applying the same discursive analytic strategy using a piece of everyday text, the Annual Barbecue flyer.

The children agreed to have Stefanie write a letter to the chair of the school barbecue expressing our concern. While drafting this letter Stefanie had a number of discussions with a group of four other children to decide what words to use. 'Why don't you say that people need food to live', Melanie suggested. 'And, ummm, if you don't eat, you'll die', PJ added. 'Should I say "have to" like it's very important?', Stefanie asked. After this discussion, Stefanie asked me if I would scribe the letter. She said that we needed to send it right away and that if she had to do drafts then it might take too long. The letter was written as follows,

> If we don't eat food we'll die.
> We have to get new hot dogs and hamburgers.
> You can ask Anthony's daddy what you can buy
> because Anthony is a vegetarian.

Stefanie began her letter by declaring, 'If we don't eat food we'll die'. The use of 'we' as opposed to 'If Anthony doesn't eat he'll die' was a deliberate choice based on a previous conversation about why a petition is a better tool for making a case for yourself than a survey. Curtis, one of the boys in the class, had concluded our discussion about petitions by saying, 'one brain is strong but lots of brains is stronger'. When I asked her why she chose 'we' over 'Anthony' she referred directly to Curtis' statement saying 'Remember Ms Vasquez ... about lots of brains?' The use of 'we', therefore, is used to symbolize strength in numbers, solidarity and inclusiveness, while in essence evaluating the organizer of the school barbecue and suggesting that the organizer do something with regards to having vegetarian food at the next barbecue. In her opening sentence she claims an implicit authority by speaking on behalf of both the reader and the speakers (the children in our class). In her letter Stefanie is adamant, using the phrase 'have to' with regards to making available vegetarian hot dogs and hamburgers. Earlier in the day PJ and Melanie also talked to Stefanie about using 'have to' as a way of telling someone you are serious. They said that saying 'please' would be polite but that it probably would not work in this situation. The word please, they said, would imply that we are asking if we can have vegetarian food at the next barbecue rather than taking a stand on the issue. According to Stefanie, 'Mostly please is good to use but not this time'.

Anthony had contributed to the letter writing by saying 'My daddy knows where to buy vegetarian food'. Stefanie felt that letting the chair know where to buy the food was a good idea because it was a way of helping solve the problem and further demonstrating how serious we really were about dealing with this issue and that we do know what we are talking about. Also, there is a sense of immediacy and an expectation for action associated with having written, 'You can ask Anthony's daddy where to buy vegetarian food' rather than 'Anthony's daddy knows where to buy vegetarian food'.

Once the letter was written, Stefanie and a friend deposited it in the inter-school mailbox. Then it was time to wait for a response. My students became increasingly frustrated with waiting. I used this waiting time as an opportunity to talk to the group about follow-up letters and sending multiple letters as two ways of showing the seriousness of your intent. I also talked to them about rereading our original letter to find better 'ways with words' to get our message across.

Stefanie decided that a follow-up letter was in order. Two weeks after sending the original letter, she had a discussion about follow-up letters with PJ, Melanie and Anthony, and then shared, with the whole group during meeting time, her intent to write a second letter. In this letter she wrote,

> *Dear Mr. Andrews,*
> *Vegetarians need food too. They*
> *don't eat meat so they can't eat at*
> *the barbecue. Because they don't*
> *eat hamburgers because they are*
> *vegetarian.*
> *Please have food for vegetarians*
> *at the next barbecue.*
> *Stefanie*
>
> *P.S. Please write me back. What happened*
> *to the letter I gave you from before?*

In the second letter Stefanie took an explicative approach by explaining what vegetarians can't eat by stating they don't eat meat, they can't eat hamburgers and they can't eat at the barbecue. In a sense she used this approach as a rationale for the position she was taking in support of vegetarians. Stefanie again made clear the seriousness of her issue and clarified the intent of her original letter by asking the chair to write back. She also made clear that this was not the first time that she had attempted to bring this issue to administrative attention. This time, however, she did receive a response. The chair of the School Barbecue Committee invited Stefanie to the office to talk about her concerns. She wrote,

> *MMM Veggie Food,*
> *Next BBQ we'll have*
> *food for vegetarians for*
> *sure. Do you have any*
> *helpful suggestions?! Come to*
> *my office soon to discuss.*
>
> *Thank you*

Encouraged, the children decided to find out more about vegetarians in order to prepare for the meeting. They turned for help to our school librarian. To their surprise they were told that there were no books about vegetarians in our library. Another letter was written. This time to the school librarian. Stefanie and her friends were learning how to make use of the critical literacies they were learning. In this letter she wrote,

> *Dear Mr. Librarian,*
> *Libraries are for kids and all people.*
> *Vegetarians are people but there's*
> *no books about them in the library.*
> *There should be books about all*
> *people in the library.*

She began her letter by stating what she knew about libraries; 'Libraries are for kids and all people'. She then used the word 'people' to link each of her sentences; libraries are for people, vegetarians are people; there should be books for all people. When I spoke with her about this she referred to the strategy as a 'pattern' like in Quick as a Cricket *and* Brown Bear, Brown Bear, *two picture books that make use of patterned text.*

As the children had expected, the librarian was very supportive of their concern and even asked Anthony if he knew of any good books that we should have in the library, as well as telling the children that he would make sure to order some books on being a vegetarian. During class meeting one day, Melissa made the comment that if at our school we 'forgot about people like vegetarians, maybe other schools did too'. Considering what she could do to find out if her hypothesis was true, and encouraged by the response Stefanie received for her letters, Melissa decided to compose her own letter to send to other elementary schools in our District. She wrote,

> *Dear Principal,*
> *We want to check that the*
> *vegetarians have food at the next*
> *barbecue in your school, if you have one.*

*Our friend couldn't eat at our
barbecue because he is a vegetarian
and that wasn't fair. Now we
want to take care that all the kids
can eat at the barbecue even the
vegetarians.*

*In her opening sentence she was explicit about the aim of the letter, which
was to find out whether there were vegetarians at the school, whether the
school had an annual barbecue and if so, was vegetarian food made available.
She put herself in a position of authority when stating 'Our friend
couldn't eat at our barbecue because he is a vegetarian and that wasn't fair'.
In adding this sentence she made it clear that she was speaking from a position
of experience. She closed her letter by re-stating her concern as an issue
of equity.*

*Melissa wanted to make sure she received a response, so I discussed with her
various options and looked at notes and letters that had previously been sent
home where parents were asked to respond in some way. She predicted the
notes with the tear away sections would be most effective. She also suspected
that if whomever answers the survey has to do too much work that they
might not respond. She told me that she knew that might happen because
her mom says, 'I don't have time for all this writing' when filling out various
forms for school. Mainly wanting to find out where other schools were in
terms of having food available for vegetarians at their school events Melissa
decided she wanted her survey 'to be just yes and no questions to check off'. I
asked her what information would be most useful to her, at which time we
worked on the questions included in her survey. The questions were: what is
the name of your school? Do you have a school barbecue? Do you know if
you have vegetarians at your school? Do you think it is fair not to have food
for vegetarians? Are you going to have food if you have vegetarians?*

*We sent out over two dozen surveys and received three responses. Of the
three responses there was consensus that none of the three schools had
thought about vegetarians being left out of school events when vegetarian
food was not made available. Each also ticked off the box saying that they
would make sure that they would have vegetarian food at future events. The
low response did not discourage the children. Their take was that they tried
something new that probably was unexpected coming from such young children
and, in spite of this, some people responded. They said that maybe next
time they'd get a better response. They were excited to have received the
responses they did and to see that the survey had worked even if only for a
limited extent. Together we talked about the possible reasons behind the low*

response. I shared my thoughts with them and they shared theirs with me. I think Melanie's comment was most enlightening. She said, 'Caring about vegetarians is not important to some people because they don't know any vegetarians. We have to just keep on helping people to get to care about people even if they don't know them'. In a way they were learning a different way of being and acting in the world.

In order to represent the vegetarian issue on our audit trail we decided to post a copy of the first letter that had been written as well as the book cover for Where the Forest Meets the Sea. *The letter reminds us of the action we took and the book cover reminds us of the connection between earlier studies regarding environmental issues and the vegetarian issue.*

The letter-writing campaign in support of vegetarians certainly brought to the fore questions regarding who else may be marginalized in some way at school. How might others be marginalized or othered because space is not provided for them? In our case it was not until 4-year-old Anthony made his comment regarding not eating at the school barbecue and his peers took social action, that the marginalization of vegetarians was brought to our awareness. There is a high probability that if the children and I had not had previous conversations regarding equity in the classroom, that Anthony's issue, which turned out to be a whole class issue, and then a school issue, would not have been noticed. To me this is a clear indication that in order to be critical, one must lead a critically literate life. I believe that it was framing our living, as a class, through critical literacy that allowed us to recognize the unfair treatment of vegetarians at our school. Taking this up as a topic for study in our curriculum led to changing the status of vegetarians in our school. Close to the end of the school year there were three social events held at our school for various reasons and different groups of people. One was the Junior Kindergarten and Senior Kindergarten Family Picnic, the other the Staff End of Year Party, and the third a birthday party for a staff member. In all three cases, vegetarian options were made available. In 12 years as a teacher with this particular school board, the option for vegetarian food was never made available at the schools where I taught.

This vignette presents a powerful example of critical literacy practices in a kindergarten classroom. The children in Vasquez's class were able to marshal the resources in hand to challenge the unquestioned practices of the school with regard to vegetarians. Throughout the activity, it was the children who were raising the important questions and identifying a range of ways to solve the problems. Vasquez's skillful guidance of this process meant that the children felt a strong sense of agency and were able to identify the discursive practices that would help them to make their case and achieve their aims. Reflecting on the principles embedded in Table 3.1, Vasquez's practice in this example can be seen to be underpinned by a number of them. Vasquez enabled children to draw on their own cultural practices and resources as they developed a response to the issue of provision for vegetarians. For example, the ability of Anthony's father to identify sources of vegetarian food was an important component of the response to the chair of the school barbecue and children drew on their knowledge of libraries as they challenged the lack of books on vegetarianism. Vasquez also encouraged children to look closely at the language used in specific texts in order to identify particular ideological stances. She facilitated children's use of literacy (in this case, primarily letter writing) as a tool to effect social change. The sequence of events, however, was not determined by her; she supported the children's choices and provided the scaffolding that enabled them to take control of the response to the situation. In this case study, Vasquez's work offers an excellent example of critical literacy as 'an evolving repertoire of practices of analysis and interrogation which move between the micro features of texts and the macro conditions of institutions, focusing upon how relations of power work through these practices' (Comber, 2003: 356).

Barbara Comber is a scholar who has written extensively on critical literacy in the early years and who has done much to support the work of researchers and teachers who are working in this field across the globe. In the following interview with Comber, we explore her responses to Vasquez's work and ask her to reflect on the role of critical literacy in primary classrooms.

INTERVIEW WITH BARBARA COMBER

WHAT ASPECTS OF THIS CASE STUDY DO YOU FEEL REFLECT THE MAIN TENETS OF CRITICAL LITERACY?

Some years ago now I argued (Comber, 1994) that there were three central principles involved in developing critical literacy pedagogy:

- repositioning students as researchers of language;

- respecting minority language practices;

- problematizing texts.

Vasquez's approach to critical literacy exemplifies all these principles. First, although she worked with children just starting their formal schooling and assembling literacy practices, she does not infantilize them; that is, she does not interact with them in ways that consign them to childish concerns or modes of practice. Vasquez does not belittle them in any way. She takes them seriously and respects their ideas, problems, questions and issues. This fundamental respect and high expectations of children's desires to inquire, to question and to learn forms the foundation of her classroom curriculum. Indeed, she elicits and fosters their serious classroom inquiries about shared interests. Starting with issues of fairness in aspects of everyday school life, such as what vegetarians might eat at the school barbecue, she leads them to discuss, inquire further and to take action. Along with the children she negotiates and designs an ambitious curriculum, available for all to see in the making, and in reflection, as part of the classroom learning wall (or audit trail). She positions the children as researchers of language practices who need to think about the decisions they make (which genres – whether they need surveys or letters or petitions), which words, what kinds of follow-up might be appropriate, and anticipate possible effects of their words. In the process, the children learn how to say what they want to say so that it will be attended to.

I have argued elsewhere that critical literacies involve people using language to exercise power, to enhance everyday life in schools and communities, and to question practices of privilege and injustice (Comber, 2001b). Teachers need to work with children's existing analytical repertoires (for example, what's fair and what isn't?), examine language artifacts and practices that contest taken-for-granted assumptions about life (for example, counter-stories, such as feminist tales, critiques of McDonald's) and offer new discursive resources (petitions, letters, surveys, critical questions). Often, teachers may claim not to have the time for critical literacy because they are concerned with the set curriculum or fear standardized tests. Vasquez's work indicates that a critical approach can begin from day one of schooling and that it is not an add-on set of curricula activities but can be integral to everyday life and learning in classrooms.

In terms of basic tenets of critical literacy, Vasquez demonstrates from the outset that literacy and language practices are not neutral and always involve power relations. Vasquez assists her students to work out: what's the problem? How can we find out more about it? What can we do about it? Who can we contact to affect change? How do we say what we want to say and make sure we get listened to? These relational aspects of institutional and everyday life are complex and political. Vasquez makes no attempt to 'protect' her young charges from this complexity. Rather she helps them to embrace, examine and understand it. At the same time she helps them to become aware that the choices they make in terms of genre and wording may make a difference to the extent to which they get responses and action. They learn words matter, but also that words have their limits.

In working with child-initiated issues, Vasquez draws children's attention to differences that make a difference in terms of participation in certain events (for example, being vegetarian, being a boy or a girl, speaking English as a second language). From the start, then, she fosters children's political awareness by allowing classroom discussions to focus on perceived injustices and processes for addressing them. This necessarily entails a critical stance towards language and literacy practices. In taking action through spoken and written language, children need to consider who can say what to whom and in what form.

WHAT DO YOU SEE AS THE MOST IMPORTANT CONTRIBUTION CRITICAL LITERACY CAN MAKE TO CLASSROOM PRACTICE?

The development of a critical literacy pedagogy and curriculum changes:

- the classroom dynamics;
- the conversations between learners and between learners and teachers;
- students' orientations to knowledge and texts.

Critical literacy ensures taken-for-granted practices, authorized texts and commonsense knowledges are subject to question. Most importantly, it creates truly dialogic spaces for young people to interrogate, question and learn about how other people think and live. From my perspective a critical literacy orientation to curriculum improves the chances that classroom work will be educative, rather than simply going through the motions and rehearsing familiar scripts. Students start to examine things in depth. A healthy scepticism is introduced at the same time as fostering children's curiosity. Over time young people can assemble a repertoire of analytical and representational resources that they take beyond the school into everyday life.

■ WHAT IDEAS DO YOU HAVE TO HELP TEACHERS UNDERSTAND THE FOUNDATIONS OF CRITICAL LITERACY?

I often begin with text analysis in helping teachers consider critical literacy for the first time. A key starting point for my work with teachers is often to critically examine the way in which they (and/or their students) are represented in the press. Unfortunately, internationally the press is rarely kind to teachers or to young people. Teachers, and their institutions, especially state-funded schools, are often portrayed as failing. Young people are typically represented as dangerous or vulnerable. The obvious unfairness of such negative representations and their consequent effects often mobilizes teachers' sometime submerged political identities and generates a desire for critical reading and answering back.

Another helpful starting point for eliciting and developing teachers' critical literacy is advertising, especially everyday texts across a variety of media. Teachers often enjoy interrogating the gender, age, locality, class and race of people depicted in television advertisements, billboards, junk mail, magazines, promotional websites and so on. They can readily see how to work with children to undertake similar critical reading. I find that teachers are willing participants in critically reading texts about which they are already sceptical. They are sometimes less enthusiastic about questioning their preferred textbooks or favourite literature. However, once they have developed some critical angles for considering texts, they can begin to apply such an approach to the literary canon or even encyclopedia. This move is harder because, as teachers, we have been invested with the responsibility of inducting young people into the authority of the text and unproblematically selling our generation's highlights to the next.

Other important points of entry for teachers into a critical approach to curriculum design and pedagogy are their own commitments to wider social issues, such as gender equity, gay rights, racial and religious tolerance, care for refugees or the war against poverty. Despite the potential of harnessing these agendas, some teachers' private politics and identity positions may well be conservative or even reactionary and not conducive to interrogating power relations or identity politics. In such cases, textual politics are relatively easier to broach, though the long-term classroom effects and take-up may be limited. Not all teachers want to lead, as Vasquez does, a critically literate life.

Another crucial and often under-explored foundational area for critical literacy work is around the design and construction of texts and/or communication practices. This involves teachers, as in the case of Vasquez, working with young people to closely examine their own texts and to imagine and anticipate the effects of their textual practices on their peers and other people. Developing critical writing pedagogy with students in classrooms needs a lot more work from school-based educators (Kamler, 2001). Sometimes an awareness of the effects of their words can begin with dramatic performances of students' writing and illustrated narratives through authors' theatre (Dyson, 1993). Other times with very young children, as Vasquez demonstrates through her Speakers' Corner, purely oral language events can be powerful sites for examining language and power. Also, working with different media, and creating visual as well as verbal texts, such as making picture books, short films, still photographs or web pages, can demonstrate to children how many decisions they need to make when producing texts in various media for various audiences (Comber and Nixon, 2004; Janks and Comber, 2005; Luke et al., 2003; Nixon and Comber, 2005). Involving young people in the processes of design, text production and editing demonstrates that texts are not neutral or natural. They can see first hand that texts are assembled by people with particular interests and motivations, and when they try out their texts on readers, audiences and viewers they can begin to get a sense of possible effects.

HOW DO YOU HELP TEACHERS IMPLEMENT A CRITICAL LITERACY FRAMEWORK IN THEIR CLASSROOMS?

I have found it useful to document, often in quite some descriptive detail, the classroom work of teachers who take a critical approach, sometimes as a co-author and sometimes writing for or alongside the teachers (Comber, 1993; 2001b; Comber et al., 2001; O'Brien and Comber, 2000). I do this primarily to make their practices available to more teachers. Although I have done quite a lot of this in print and in video format (for example, Hill et al., 1994), I still feel that it has limited effects. I also work with lots of teachers at conferences and in workshops. The most effective work I believe I have done around implementation has been to set up long-term connections with teacher-researchers and assist them to document their work in various media and organize different kinds of dissemination. Sometimes this has been funded by grants; at other times done through sheer goodwill and after-hours labour or by researchers and teachers. Another key site for this work is through graduate and undergraduate teacher education. When teachers have the opportunity to study 'critical literacy' as a concept with a history and try out and adapt their practices, rather than simply adopting sets of techniques, it has more sustainable effects, as was the case for Vasquez.

I believe that the authorization of critical literacy in policy and curriculum is another key way to ensure that its implementation goes beyond a few radical zealots. However, along with that comes the risk of its being made safer, schooled and domesticated. In Australia, several states have incorporated a critical perspective into their literacy curricula, particularly taking up Freebody and Luke's four roles (1990) heuristic and developing guides to text analysis (see Comber and Simpson, 1995; Education Queensland, 2000). However, little follow-up research has been done to ascertain the extent to which these text-analytic practices have been taken up in schools, and standardized texts still tend to privilege a familiar approach to comprehension and grammar.

WHAT ARE THE IMPLICATIONS OF CRITICAL LITERACY FOR LITERACY RESEARCH IN THE CONTEMPORARY CONTEXT?

It is getting harder to win funding to do the kinds of research in critical literacy that need to be done. Funding priorities right now seem to be around normative or standardized literacy, rather than more expansive views of literacy. Recently, with a large team of experienced educational researchers, I unsuccessfully applied for funding to explore critical literacy pedagogies in various locations internationally. If we had been successful, teams of university and school-based researchers would have worked together to closely document their practices and the effects on different students. We would have focused on the classroom discourse in different critical literacy classrooms; the kinds of assignments set, negotiated and accomplished; and the different response and take-up of different students within classrooms and across classrooms. These areas remain relatively unexplored and, in my view, require a lot more careful investigation than certainly I have been able to accomplish thus far. Moreover, we had planned to make these practices available to other educators through a purpose-built web site. In this case we did not get the grant. So it is back to the drawing board to consider how we can operate more strategically whilst maintaining our commitment to critical literacy.

We need more accounts by teachers like Vasquez (Vasquez, 2001; 2004a) and perhaps more by collectives of practitioners and academics working together for social justice through literacy. Perhaps one way to attract funding to ongoing pedagogical work in critical literacy is to prioritize the study of the emergence of new literacies, especially young people's learning to work and play with ICT and various media. Such an approach might capitalize on the anxieties that exist around the supposed fascination and facility of young people with new technologies, and government and private industry's huge investments in these in workplaces, leisure and services. New research in critical literacies, I think, needs to go beyond text analysis and tackle a range of social and textual practices that contest unequal power relations and symbolic violence in various sites.

CONCLUSION

This chapter has explored the nature of critical literacy and offered a theoretical framework for practice. The case study illustrated the way in which children can engage in classroom activities that are purposeful and offer opportunities to critique the normalized discourses that pervade educational institutions. The interview with Comber further emphasized the importance of enhancing children's critical skills through the development of curricula and pedagogy that challenge traditional, hegemonic practices and provide an appropriate education for a socially just society (see also Lingard, 2005). In the next chapter, we move on to consider questions relating to educational provision in a rapidly changing world, for not only do we need to consider pedagogical practices that are critical in nature and promote social justice, but we also urgently need curricula that reflect twenty-first century social practices, rooted as these are in technological transformations.

NOTES

1   It is beyond the scope of this chapter to review the field of critical pedagogy, although it is closely related to issues of critical literacy. For further explication and critique of critical pedagogy, see: Giroux (1988); Shor (1992; 1996).

2   This description is taken from Vasquez (2004a), used with permission from the publisher.

CHAPTER 4

Literacy and New Technologies

New information and communication technologies have changed, irrevocably, the nature and use of literacy. Kress (2003) suggests that there are two particular factors which have impacted on the nature of literacy in a new media age:

> *These are, on the one hand, the broad move from the now centuries-long dominance of writing to the new dominance of the image and, on the other hand, the move from the dominance of the medium of the book to the dominance of the medium of the screen. These two together are producing a revolution in the uses and effects of literacy and of associated means for representing and communicating at every level and in every domain. (Kress, 2003: 1)*

Over the past decade, Kress and other literacy researchers (Carrington, 2004; Lankshear and Knobel, 2003a; 2004a; 2004b; Nixon and Comber, 2005) have been making the point that this digital turn has happened and we have not paid attention. In this chapter, we review some of the main issues and concepts in the field, outline educational practice that incorporates digital literacy practices in the primary classroom and close with an interview with Michele Knobel and Colin Lankshear in which they outline their reflections on current and future theory, research and practice in the field.

HISTORICAL AND THEORETICAL GROUND

Changes in literacy practices precipitated by the developments in technology have been so profound that they have challenged our understanding of the very nature of literacy itself. Some researchers have responded to these changes by pluralizing the term 'literacy' in order to account for multiple ways of making meaning; 'multiliteracies' is a commonly used term (Cope and Kalantzis, 2000). In addition, the term 'literacy' has been wedded to a range of other nouns and adjectives in attempts to convey competence in a range of areas. However, although the phrases 'media literacy' or 'digital literacy' appear to be widely accepted (Buckingham, 2003), Kress (2003: 23–4) suggests that the term 'literacy' should relate to lettered representation and that other uses of the word have conflated representational modes and their related resources of production and dissemination (2003: 23). Nevertheless, whilst Kress's work in many ways throws clear light on the subject, it has to be accepted that the use of the term 'literacy' to refer to competence in various aspects of new technologies is so widespread that to rein in the meaning would appear to be an impossible task. Certainly, in the discussion of the impact of new technologies on literacy, the phrases 'digital literacy' (Glister, 1997), 'new literacies' (Lankshear and Knobel, 2003a), 'media literacy' (Buckingham, 2003) and 'moving image literacy' (Burn and Leach, 2004) all have currency and appear to address similar issues, namely, the ability to decode, encode and make meaning using a range of modes of communication including print, still and moving image, sound and gesture, all mediated by new technologies.

Marsh (2003a) has suggested one model which enables a focus on literacy as 'lettered representation', but which also acknowledges the way in which current practices involve much more than a focus on printed text. Figure 4.1 presents a map of the relationship between various meaning-making practices and events. Here, the term 'communication' provides the overarching concept which encompasses a range of ways of making meaning, including literacy (Street, 1997). The distinction is made between communicative practices and events (Barton, 1994). As stated in Chapter 3, practices are the overarching sociocultural systems from which we draw in any communicative event. So, for example, as we write a letter to a family member (a literacy event), we draw from the cultural systems which situate letter-writing as a social practice amongst family members (a literacy practice) (Barton and Hamilton, 1998). The dotted arrows in Figure 4.1 indicate this relationship between practices and events.

In Figure 4.1, it can be seen that communicative practices and events include written, oral, visual and corporeal forms of making-meaning. The solid arrows indicate the interface between the different modes of communication. Any event may involve one or more communicative forms. For example, the act of a young child reading a picture storybook can be a visual, literate, oral and corporeal event.

Figure 4.1, therefore, offers one way of analyzing the interaction between literacy and other communicative modes. Whatever the model one adopts, there is certainly a need to reconsider traditional notions of literacy, given

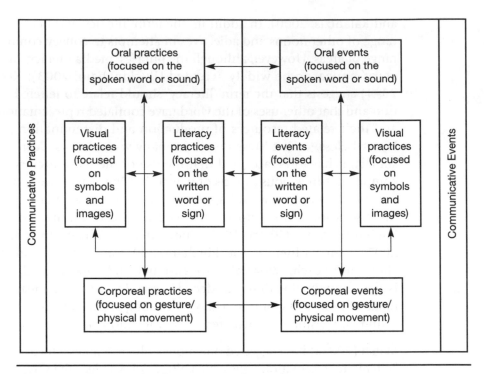

Figure 4.1 Communicative events and practices

the range and nature of childrens' and young people's communicative practices outside of school. These now involve a wide range of media such as television, DVDs, computers, handheld computers, mobile phones and console games (Knobel and Lankshear, 2003; Livingstone and Bovill, 1999). Children become competent in using these digital technologies from a very young age (Marsh, 2004b; Marsh and Thompson, 2001; Rideout et al., 2003) and the lack of attention by educators to this experience creates dissonance between home and school experiences from children's first years of schooling (Knobel and Lankshear, 2003; Marsh, 2003a). Lankshear and Knobel (2003a; 2004a) suggest that this gap between in- and out-of school experiences for some children is so great that the ICT activities offered in school appear tame by comparison, and this can lead to disaffection and disengagement:

> *To be sure, pedagogy and curriculum cannot be 'hostaged' to every change in cultural tools and uses that appear on the horizon. At the same time, if limits to learners' affinities, allegiances, identities and prior experience are transgressed beyond a certain point, even 'successful' learners (with the right cultural and social capital) will decline the offers made by formal education. (Lankshear and Knobel, 2004a: np)*

Given the inevitable gap between the fast-moving developments in technology in society and the acquisition of the relevant hardware and software by cash-strapped schools, there is never going to be perfect synergy between the two domains. However, schools could be doing more to address the issues and much of the curricula and pedagogical changes would need to be underpinned by an understanding of the epistemological and ontological changes precipitated by the digital paradigm shift (Lankshear and Knobel, 2003a).

IMPLICATIONS FOR CLASSROOMS

The developments in relation to new technologies have a number of significant implications for pedagogy. In the following sections, we consider the impact these changes have had on the nature of the reading and writing process in relation to the 'digitextual practices' (Everett, 2003: 5) of learners, and then move on to consider the implications for the role of the teacher.

LEARNERS

Lankshear and Knobel (2004b) identify four roles which they suggest characterize the practices people engage in as they learn to produce, distribute and exchange texts in a new media age. Using the phrase the 'digitally at home' to describe a generation comfortable with and competent in the use of new technologies, the roles they outline for these digitally at home are a 'designer' of texts, a text 'mediator' or 'broker', a text 'bricoleur' and a text 'jammer' (Lankshear and Knobel, 2004b). These categories are not intended to be exhaustive; they serve as examples of the kinds of roles assumed by authors of digital texts.

With regard to the role of 'text designer', Lankshear and Knobel (2004b) emphasize that the concept of design, rather than traditional conceptions of authorship, is important in the production of multimodal, digital texts. This has also been a constant theme in the work of Gunther Kress over the last decade (1997; 2003). Kress suggests that: 'Design takes for granted competence in the use of resources, but beyond that it requires the orchestration and remaking of these resources in the service of frameworks and models that express the maker's intentions in shaping the social and cultural environment' (Kress, 1997: 77). This has implications for teachers in that an understanding is needed of the ways in which such decision-making processes can be supported and extended. In addition, recognition of the range of resources children draw on as they make these decisions needs to be developed within nurseries and schools. Educators who have a broader understanding of the rich range of textual practices children bring to the classroom have greater opportunities to enhance children's learning (Dyson, 1997; 2002).

In addition to 'text designer', Lankshear and Knobel also identify the role of text 'bricoleur' as being significant to contemporary communicative practices. Lankshear and Knobel elicit de Certau's concept of bricolage as being the 'artisant like inventiveness' (de Certeau, 1984: xv, 66) of people's everyday practices in which they draw on whatever is to hand to create texts. Lankshear and Knobel illustrate the concept by focusing on web users' creation of texts within online communities. Of course, this intertextual aspect of children's texts is not particular to new technologies; as the work of Dyson indicates in relation to children's paper-based writing tasks, Bahktinian principles of heteroglossia and dialogical processes permeate children's classroom work (Dyson, 1997; 2002). However, the use of new media does make this bricolage process much easier and it is clear that a key role for the educator in the information economy is to facilitate children's development of critical literacy skills in relation to web-based material (Lankshear and Knobel, 2003a), so that children can effectively undertake the authorial role of 'text bricoleur'.

The third role Lankshear and Knobel (2004b) identify is that of 'text broker'. In relation to new media practices, this could describe, for example, the role of people who manage discussion boards, or people who give online articles and blogs (online web diaries) ratings so that readers have guidance, should they want this, in terms of which texts they should read. The broker mediates texts between the author and reader. Finally, the role of 'text jammer' describes the process of changing or adapting electronic texts in order to subvert the messages given – in effect, online critical literacy practices. All these roles present challenges for the usual practices of primary classrooms, in which authorial roles in relation to texts are generally restricted to normative conceptions of what a 'writer' does. In the following section, we explore the implications of the textual practices of the 'digitally at home' (Lankshear and Knobel, 2004b) for the teacher.

TEACHERS

Many older teachers did not grow up using technology extensively and a number of researchers have suggested that this has created a situation in which educators are positioned as 'newcomers' or 'outsiders' to technology, whilst children and young people constitute the 'insiders' (Lankshear and Bigum, 1999). Whilst the situation is, no doubt, more complex in that some teachers will be confident with technology and a number of children placed on the edges of digital practices because of lack of access to technology at home (Holloway and Valentine, 2003), there is a generation gap which means that many teachers experience discomfort and anxiety in relation to ICT and literacy (Carrington, 2004; Turbill, 2001).

Whilst many of the traditional roles of a teacher would be maintained in a new media age, such as teacher as facilitator, instructor, model and so on, we would suggest that there are three additional roles teachers need to adopt in order to facilitate children's navigation of complex, multimodal, electronic worlds. These can be conceptualized in the following way:

- Teacher as *resource manager*. This involves providing children with a range of resources that can enable them to develop the skills, knowledge and understanding needed to analyse and produce multimodal, multimedia texts. However, it is not simply a matter of provision; indeed, children themselves can bring valuable resources to the site of learning, given their knowledge of such resources, such as websites, outside of school. Rather, the teacher needs to ensure that, overall, resources are sufficiently broad and balanced to facilitate effective learning. In addition, the teacher needs to enable children to develop further their critical skills in relation to resources, helping children to make decisions about the affordances of different modes and media so that they can use these appropriately.

- Teacher as *co-constructor of knowledge*. There has been much already written about how, in a new media age, the role of teacher needs to move from one of possessing authoritative knowledge to acknowledging that students will know as much, if not more, at times and so an effective pedagogical model is one of teachers and students learning together (Lankshear and Knobel, 2003a).

- Teacher as *design consultant*. If one of the key authorial roles children adopt in a new media age is that of 'text designer' (Lankshear and Knobel, 2004b), then an important role for the teacher becomes one in which advice and feedback is given on the processes and products of designs. Consultancy assumes some sort of expertise on the part of the consultant. In this case, the expectation is not that the teacher would have a much broader knowledge of the range of electronic texts that children may analyse or produce; the opposite may, in fact, be the case, given children's encounters with a multitude of texts outside of classrooms (Livingstone and Bovill, 1999). Rather, the expertise would be related to the knowledge teachers have of curriculum and assessment frameworks and one of her or his main aims would be to ensure that children's work helped them to meet these specific criteria. Feedback on design processes or products, therefore, would be predicated on an understanding of the kinds of skills, knowledge and understanding children need to demonstrate in order to meet externally imposed criteria. In addition, consultancy usually involves an appraisal by the consultant of the areas that the 'client' has not already considered and feedback on this; similarly, teachers need to provide advice to pupils on aspects of the assignment or product that have been overlooked. Often, this task is made easier in relation to technology-based activities, as children can track decision-making processes in a more transparent manner because of the affordances of the electronic mode (for example, the ability to save different versions). Finally, a consultancy role is usually one in which the agenda is firmly within the hands of the 'client'; he or she decides what the particular issue or problem is that requires a consultant's input. Similarly, in literacy activities involving new technologies, children need to be encouraged by teachers to make the kind of reflective decisions that lead to self-identification of issues for further consultation.

This list is not exhaustive; our intent is not to provide a definitive set of roles which characterize literacy teaching in a new media age. However, it is indicative of the kinds of changes that are needed if literacy education in primary classrooms is to change in an appropriate manner for the range of textual practices in which children now engage. Burnett et al. (2004) suggest that there are often two conceptions of curriculum and pedagogical change, particularly within the UK, offered in relation to new media education:

> *Two contrasting paradigms characterize current curriculum policy in the UK with respect to new technology. The 'blue sky thinking' of the government's e-learning strategy envisions a future in which teaching and learning are transformed, schools become new sorts of learning environments, and curricula mutate accordingly (...). At the same time, the work of the Primary National Strategy and the Key Stage Three Strategy adopts an 'enrichment' view of new technology, in which Smart Boards replace blackboards and websites replace worksheets. (Burnett et al., 2004: 1)*

This dichotomy, enrichment or transformation, is an important one to consider, given the very real constraints on practice in many classrooms, with limited budgets and lack of teacher expertise or confidence in new technologies. However, if technology is viewed simply as an 'add-on' by teachers, a means to enhance what is a traditional model of literacy pedagogy, then children will not develop the range of skills and knowledge they need in contemporary societies. Instead, Lankshear and Knobel (2004a) argue that educative practice needs to be thoroughly transformed to reflect four key principles of learning: the principle of efficacious learning, the principle of integrated learning, the principle of productive appropriation and extension in learning, and the principle of critical learning. In Table 4.1, we outline Lankshear and Knobel's principles, define each of these principles using terminology from Lankshear and Knobel's paper and, in the final column, add reflections of our own about the implications of these principles for the role of the teacher.

Table 4.1 Lankshear and Knobel's (2004a) four principles of learning

Principle	Description (from Lankshear and Knobel, 2004a)	Implications for the role of the teacher
The principle of efficacious learning	Learning should be connected in meaningful ways to learners' social and cultural practices. Learning should be inseparable from Discourses (Gee, 1996).	Needs to be responsive to the discursive worlds of learners and provide meaningful opportunities for learning which integrate with these worlds.
The principle of integrated learning	Integrated learning is situated inside a practice and relates to our identities. Learning is holistic and organic; it does not consist of learning 'chunks' in isolation from the Discourse as a whole.	Needs to understand the way in which Discourses are constructed and provide learning opportunities that are integrated.
The principle of productive appropriation and extension in learning	The process of learning should not involve conflict between social identities. Learning should provide opportunities for learners to transfer specific discursive practices into new spaces.	Needs to enable learners to bring their 'funds of knowledge' (Moll et al., 1992) to the site of learning.
The principle of critical learning	Learners should experience different and competing Discourses and be able to navigate critically these contested spaces.	Needs to provide opportunities for learners to experience and respond critically to a range of discursive practices, identities, texts and so on.

In many ways, these four principles of learning should underpin pedagogical work in activities not mediated by new technologies. However, Lankshear and Knobel (2003a; 2004a; 2004b) argue that new social and textual practices are changing in an accelerated manner to such an extent that unless schools do urgently adopt these principles, they will become even more anachronistic and outmoded than has been the case in previous generations. Nevertheless, despite these major reservations about the current context, there has been some work that has explored the potential that new technologies have for the transformation of the literacy curriculum. In the following section, we provide a brief overview of some of the emerging issues.

IMPLICATIONS FOR RESEARCHING LITERACY

So far, we have considered the nature of technological changes in relation to learners and educators. In this section, we will explore the implications these changes have for a future research agenda in literacy. One of the foremost considerations of future research in the field must be the nature of the curriculum needed for contemporary life, given that literacy practices are now: 'less exclusively related to lexicosyntactic text and more to a foreground of complex iconography of pictures, symbols, moving images and sound embedded in a background environment (and complex cultural and political economy) of global connectivity' (Luke, 2003: 22).

Often, research undertaken in relation to new technologies has not been sited within the literacy curriculum, but related to media education. From research conducted within educational settings, it is clear that media analysis and production does lead to the development of a range of literacy-related skills, knowledge and understanding. For example, in a review of 12 studies that focused on moving image education, Burn and Leach (2004) identified four emergent patterns, patterns that indicated the benefits to be gained from such work: (1) moving image work is located within the sociocultural interests and experiences of children and young people; (2) work on moving image media leads to gains in literacy (broadly defined); (3) media production can be a collaborative process and (4) working with moving image media is motivational. In a report on a project in which 50 schools in the UK introduced digital filming and editing into the curriculum (Reid et al., 2002) the authors found that introducing work on moving image media supported the development of a range of transferable skills, including, 'problem-solving, negotiation, thinking, reasoning and risk-taking' (Reid et al., 2002: 3). In addition, they determined that the opportunities afforded by animation work were strong because of the way in which children could combine voice, gesture, music, image and language. However, this kind of work is relatively under-explored within a primary context and there needs to be more extensive research that can illuminate the educational benefits of work on moving image.

Video games are another source of interest for literacy researchers. Evidence suggests that playing computer games is a favourite leisure activity outside of school. Livingstone and Bovill's survey of 1,303 children in the UK aged 6–17 notes that 64 per cent of children across all age groups play computer games during their leisure time and that they play, on average, for 34 minutes per day. The 'Young People and Media 2002' survey (Hayward et al., 2002) identified a difference between younger and older children in relation to game-playing. Of the 592 primary-aged children questioned, 88 per cent stated that they used a computer to play games. In the TEEM project (McFarlane et al., 2002), 800 questionnaires were distributed to pupils in 12 primary and secondary schools and over 700 were completed. The findings suggest that the majority of the children surveyed played games at home, usually in their bedrooms. Approximately 25 per cent of pupils stated that they played games for over two hours at a time and half the children surveyed reported that they played games through the Internet. The TEEM data also demonstrated that children were more likely to play games with one or more friends than play on their own. The social aspect of computer games-playing has also been identified in other studies (Facer et al., 2003).

The TEEM report (McFarlane et al., 2002) outlines a range of skills, knowledge and understanding that respondents felt computer games developed. Children were asked what they felt they learned from playing computer games. Twenty-five percent of children in primary schools felt that playing games helped to develop their general knowledge and helped with school subjects. Teachers identified a range of skills, knowledge and understanding that they felt were developed through the use of computer games. These included problem-solving skills and communication skills. In addition, teachers felt that games contributed to the development of the following subject areas: (1) personal and social development (motivation, attention and group skills); (2) language and literacy (listening skills, using talk to organize, sequence and clarify thinking); (3) mathematical development (language for positioning, application of number); (4) creative development (music, art and design, use of imagination); (5) knowledge and understanding of the world (control software to investigate direction and control); (6) physical development (fine motor control) (McFarlane et al., 2002: 13–14). Previous research has also suggested that computer games develop logical thinking, problem-solving skills and parallel processing (Dawes and Dumbelton, 2001; Greenfield, 1984; Greenfield and Cocking, 1994) and some researchers have purported that this learning is transferable to other contexts (Whitebread, 1997). In addition, studies have suggested that hand/eye co-ordination and spatial skills are developed as children manipulate figures and objects on screen (Gagnon, 1985; Greenfield, 1984; Loftus and Loftus, 1983). Further, there is work which suggests that playing computer games can develop children's understanding of narrative structure (Berger, 2000). This research has been keen to identify the generic or transferable skills that game-playing is said to develop. However, there is a more recent body of work focusing on the unique environments of computer games that suggests that learners develop skills specific to that domain which should be adopted in other domains.

Prensky (2001) has argued that the use of computer games produces a specific 'games literacy' that involves changes in skills and educational process from more traditional forms of ICT, as shown in Table 4.2.

Table 4.2 Changes in skills and processes (Prensky, 2003)

Conventional speed	to	Twitch speed
Linear processing	to	Parallel processing
Step by step	to	Random access
Text first	to	Graphics first
Work-oriented	to	Play-oriented
Stand-alone	to	Connected

He purports that the specific attributes of computer games lead to increased motivation for learners and that this aspect of games has been ignored by educators (Prensky, 2003). Gee (2003) also argues for the recognition of the unique educational environment of computer gaming. He suggests that there are a number (36) of learning principles embedded within computer game design that promote critical thinking and that could be usefully embedded within educational programs. These learning principles include the 'semiotic domains principle', which suggests that learning involves the ability to participate in affinity groups linked to particular domains. This relates to the work identified earlier, emphasizing the social nature of game-playing as much as the educational nature (Facer et al., 2003). However, a recent review of the literature on games and learning (Kirriemuir and McFarlane, 2004) points out that much of the work which presents claims for the educational benefits of computer games is not empirically based:

*To date, however, it could be argued that much of this research relies on infer-
ence from the structure of computer games and psychological theory rather
than direct and sustained empirical evidence. Recent studies at NESTA
Futurelab have raised some questions as to whether children are in fact able
to move from intuitive problem solving in the game to an understanding of
effective processes for identifying problems and generating hypotheses and
solutions in other contexts. (Kirriemuir and McFarlane, 2004: 14)*

This is obviously an area which needs further research before any claims
can be made about the impact of computer game-playing on literacy practices. However, it is clear that video games offer a myriad of learning
opportunities and the models of learning embedded within them could be
usefully adopted by producers of educational software (Gee, 2003).

Although this is still an emerging field, there are a number of principles
that can be applied to a consideration of the nature of literacy in a new
media age. These can be seen in Table 4.3.

Table 4.3 **Principles of literacy learning in a new media age**

1. Teachers need to be aware of the implications of the changing nature of literacy
    in that word and image are becoming more specialized in terms of their
    functions in texts (Kress, 2003).

2. The historical shift from an emphasis on word to image has been accompanied
    by a move from book to screen, which has implications for the kinds of texts we
    privilege in schools (Kress, 2003).

3. Schools have traditionally focused on print-based texts, however, the texts children
    encounter outside of school are increasingly multimodal in nature and teachers,
    therefore, need to understand key concepts of multimodality (Kress, 2003).

4. Learners need to develop skills in relation to the design, production and analysis
    of multimodal texts (Kress, 2003; Lankshear and Knobel, 2004b).

5. Teachers need to develop an understanding of the needs of learners as children
    construct, deconstruct and respond to multimodal texts. Pedagogical shifts are
    needed if teaching and learning are to develop in ways appropriate for a
    technological age (Lankshear and Knobel, 2003a; 2004a; 2004b).

6. Technology should not be used simply to replicate traditional literacy practices.
    The affordances of various hardware and software need to be utilized effectively
    and the resources used to analyse and produce a range of multimodal texts
    (Lankshear and Knobel, 2003a). The principle should be *transformation* of
    curricula and pedagogy rather than *enrichment* (Burnett et al., 2004).

Although some of the work outlined does provide indicative evidence of the potential new technologies have within the classroom context, there are few empirical accounts of such work that can serve to inform primary teachers' practice. In the following section, we describe the classroom practice of Hilary Malden, a primary school teacher in England.

CLASSROOM CASE STUDY: HILARY MALDEN, SHEFFIELD, UK

CONTEXT

Hilary Malden is a teacher at Meersbrook Bank Primary School in Sheffield, England. Malden qualified as a teacher in 1979 and taught at several different primary schools before joining Meersbrook Bank. The school is located in the city and is typical of many inner-city English primary schools in that it is situated in a large, rambling Victorian building. Pupils attending the school have a wide variety of racial and linguistic heritages and the socioeconomic status of the families whose children attend the school is also varied. Malden teaches 24 pupils aged 9 and 10 in Year 5, the penultimate year in primary school. She undertook a Masters degree some years ago, but has not undertaken any specific training in the use of information and communication technologies (ICT). Indeed, she describes herself as, 'not a computer whiz. I've never been an ICT specialist. It's just that we have a new head who is an expert in ICT and he has given a lead and developed our confidence to have a go'. One of the key features of this case study, as will become clear, is that it could describe many primary classrooms in the UK and elsewhere. There are no special ICT resources, no additional training or infrastructure which marks it out from other contexts. This was, we felt, important in describing work that is embedded in new technologies. It would be too easy to use specialist schools that have developed ICT across the curriculum in hotbeds of innovation, but this might provide an opportunity for readers to feel that it is so removed from their contexts that they could not relate to the work being described. Instead, we feature the classroom of Hilary Malden, a dedicated and talented teacher, but one who is working within the constraints of restricted budgets and competing government demands for training and development. Thus, the practice described does not utilize the most advanced of technologies, but relies on digital cameras, presentation software and a standard email package.[1]

PHYSICAL ENVIRONMENT AND RESOURCES

Malden's classroom is fairly typical of many primary classrooms in England in that it has only two computers available for the children on a permanent basis. Although Malden plans for these so that they are constantly in use by children, the amount of work which can be conducted on them is limited. The school does not have laptops that can be used by children within individual classrooms. This would be, Malden acknowledges, a useful addition that would enable children to extend their skills, knowledge and understanding much further. The classroom does contain an interactive whiteboard, which is linked to Malden's laptop, provided by the school. Malden takes this laptop home on a regular basis in order to prepare for the next day's use of the interactive whiteboard. She also uses the laptop for her curriculum planning.

In addition to the specific ICT resources within classrooms, the school has a computer suite. This is a room that has 12 networked computers, in addition to an interactive whiteboard. The room is used for whole-class lessons and all classes in the school have timetabled sessions in the suite. Malden is timetabled for two lessons a week in the suite. As suggested earlier, it is clear from this description that this class is fairly typical of many primary classrooms in that it is not spectacularly well resourced for ICT. However, despite the lack of extensive ICT resources, Malden manages to develop a literacy curriculum which extends traditional models of practice.

THE CURRICULUM

The school curriculum is guided by the requirements of the National Curriculum (DfES/QCA, 1999). In addition to the National Curriculum guidance, the school draws on the Qualifications and Curriculum Authority's (QCA) schemes of work and the Primary Strategy materials. This means that, in effect, there is quite strong classification and framing in relation to the curriculum (Bernstein, 2000). It is clear that developments in England over the past eight years in terms of a return to quite rigid curriculum structures have facilitated against incorporating children's out-of-school interests, related to new technologies, into the curriculum. In his later work, Bernstein developed the concept of horizontal and vertical discourses in order to analyze the way in which knowledge is structured in different fields. A horizontal discourse refers to 'everyday, oral or common-sense knowledge: and is one in which knowledge is not structured in a hierarchical fashion, instead it is ... local, segmental, context pendent, tacit, multi-layered, often contradictory across contexts but not within contexts'

(Bernstein, 1996: 170). A vertical discourse, on the other hand, 'takes the form of a coherent, explicit, systematically principled structure, hierarchically organised, or it takes the form of a series of specialized criteria for the production of texts' (Bernstein, 1996: 171). Bernstein's concepts of horizontal and vertical knowledge posit a clear distinction between schooled and out-of school forms of knowledge. Moss argues that such a distinction means that informal and schooled literacies are incompatible:

> Informal literacies create different kinds of knowledge structures from schooled literacies, tied to the exigencies of the present moment ... They are regulated quite differently from official literacies, which bring with them instituionalised trappings of schooling. Precisely because of the differences such modes of regulation engender, informal literacies do not act as a powerful resource within school settings. (Moss, 2000: 62)

Whilst this analysis certainly indicates why informal literacy practices do not integrate easily within the official curriculum, it does not explain how such resources can and do provide a powerful resource within schools, a resource that children recontextualize and embed in organic ways into the everyday literacy curriculum (Dyson, 1997; 2001a; 2001b; 2002). Certainly, in her curriculum planning, Malden uses the curriculum framework as a springboard for her work and does not feel that it necessarily restricts her practice to such an extent that it does not enable her to incorporate children's social practices into the literacy curriculum. In addition, despite the National Literacy Strategy Framework's (DfEE, 1998) initial lack of attention to the way in which new technologies and media have impacted on literacy (Marsh, 2004a), Malden embeds technology in an integral way into her planning for literacy.

In her subject planning, Malden considers whether or not technology can enhance children's learning of a particular concept or objective and, if it can, plans for its use. For example, Malden uses specifically designed software to explore aspects of literacy and language using the interactive whiteboard. One program provides a pull-down screen which can be used to cover parts of individual words, so that children have to make informed guesses based on phonemic and syllabic patterns. It can also be used to cover the end of stories so that prediction skills are developed. Other programs allow children to develop and use word banks for writing. However, these are examples of ICT being used to develop standard objectives with regard to literacy. Although effective in enhancing motivation and promoting engagement in tasks by groups and the whole class, they do not extend the parameters of literacy as a subject. These would be examples of the way in which technology can enrich literacy learning, rather than transform it, as suggested by Burnett et al. (2004). However, Malden does use the whiteboard in more innovative ways in her curriculum planning.

In her daily classroom routines, Malden embeds technology within everyday literacy lesson planning. For example, in whole-class sessions, Malden uses an interactive whiteboard to achieve specific learning objectives. At times, she focuses on developing children's self-assessment skills and their abilities to understand and enhance the revision process in writing. For this purpose, she will scan in examples of children's writing and display this on the whiteboard for all to see. These pieces of work are then used to illustrate particular points, with electronic markers utilized to highlight particular parts of the text in order to facilitate discussion. Children's work that is scanned in and displayed on the interactive whiteboard is also used to celebrate achievements, share particularly strong features and develop comprehension skills.

The whiteboard can also provide a means for whole-class composition of texts. When Malden's class create stories or poems together using the whiteboard, they can print off multiple copies so that each child has a copy of the work. The whiteboard is also used by small groups of children for similar purposes. For example, Malden recently introduced a topic on the Victorian age. Groups of children worked at the whiteboard, using it to access the Internet and examine census information for the Victorian period. They used this information to build up details about particular people, creating composite profiles of them. They also examined websites relating to child labour in Victorian times, using this information to inform journalistic writing on the topic. Malden feels that it is important for the children to develop further skills which help them to analyse critically the information they find on the web. The groups used the information they had gathered from their Internet investigations to develop electronic presentations about the Victorian age. Children regularly use presentation software to develop presentations on specific subjects. They download images from the Internet to import into their presentations, record sound effects and voice-overs and play around with the special effects. These presentations can then be placed on the web in an easy-to-access format. Although in this particular instance the focus was on history, Malden emphasizes that literacy underpins cross-curricular activities and so used the opportunity provided by this topic to develop technology-mediated literacy skills such as information retrieval and processing, organization of data and design of screens.

KEY FEATURES OF PRACTICE

One aspect of Malden's practice which deserves particular mention is the use of ICT to develop peer and self-assessment. Each child has a folder on the network that contains his or her work, created over time. These folders enable children to save work and to return to it over a period of time. However, Malden also uses the folders as a means of developing the children's ability to examine their work critically and respond to peer suggestions.

Children are paired with partners and given guidance on the criteria to use for assessing each other's work. Although this practice can, and is, carried out in relation to print-based texts, it is easier for the children to do this using computers because of the benefits of the shared screen and the ability to use specific features of software, such as the 'Comments' facility in Word.

A further aspect of Hilary's practice which deserves mention is her emphasis on children's development of ICT skills in a way which embeds those skills into subject-specific concerns. This means that the ICT skills have a meaningful application from the start. For example, in order to enable children's peer review of written work, children are taught file management skills at the same time in order to ensure that they know how to save work, rename files, copy and delete files, and so on.

ANALYSIS OF A SERIES OF LESSONS ON A THEME

In this section, we outline what happened in a project that was developed by Malden in partnership with researchers at a local university – Cathy Burnett, Paul Dickinson, Guy Merchant and Julia Myers. This project built upon previous work initiated by Guy Merchant, a researcher who has focused on exploring the implications of the teaching and learning of writing on screen in a new media age (Merchant, 2001; 2004). Merchant worked initially with Malden on a project in which he acted as a 'remote writing advisor' to children in Malden's class as they emailed him their plans for, and drafts of, stories. The collaboration worked so well that Guy went on to work more intensively with Malden's class, this time engaging in email correspondence with children as they planned and developed local myths (Merchant, 2005). In these exchanges, Merchant adopted various persona – journalist, old man, museum curator – in order to provide additional information about local history that could be used to enrich the children's stories. The children eventually published their myths on a website.

Developing the work further, Merchant involved colleagues in his research centre at the university in the planning of a project that would involve children from two schools using email to collaborate on a joint presentation. The presentation was to be focused on young children's cultural interests and practices, and was to be delivered to a group of student teachers at the university, in order to inform their understanding of contemporary childhoods. In the first stage of the project, the intention was to provide children with email partners from another school and the children would then share their own cultural interests and practices before embarking on the development of a co-authored presentation. The team approached Meersbrook Bank Primary School and invited them to take part in the project, along with another school, which was, in contrast, a small rural school. Malden became involved because she was extremely enthusiastic about the project when it was outlined to her. In addition, her work with Merchant over the previous years had developed her confidence in approaching such projects and she was keen to extend her own understanding of new literacy practices further. As well as sharing the team's interest in expanding traditional notions of literacy, Malden wanted to provide opportunities for particular children in her class to develop self-esteem through involvement in a project that would provide them with individual attention. In addition, although the class was familiar with and used email, it had never been involved in a project in which the children communicated with pupils in other schools, and this was of great interest to Hilary in extending the virtual boundaries of her classroom.

Six children from each class were chosen to take part in the project. The parents of the children in the class were contacted and all agreed that their children could be involved. The researchers decided to use the university's email network and the children in both schools were given passwords. The children in Malden's class were then assigned partners of the same gender from the other school, at which point they identified aliases. One of the key concepts of the project was the development of a 'digital shoebox' that would provide a means for children to collect together artifacts and texts which, in some way, represented aspects of their identities and life histories. This idea was developed from the use of shoeboxes to facilitate home–school communication in the ESRC Home-Exchange Project (Greenough et al. (forthcoming)). In that project, children were asked to fill a shoebox with items that represented particular aspects of themselves or their lives. These were then taken to school and used to inform oral and written activities. In Malden's class, children were asked to collect items in a shoebox. However, in this case, the children then took digital photographs of these items in order to share them via email with partners in the second school. Figures 4.2 and 4.3 provide examples of the shoeboxes of two children.

Figure 4.2 Contents of a digital shoebox

Figure 4.3 Contents of a second digital shoebox

Images of individual items in the shoebox were shared by the email partners. These then formed the basis for discussion between the partners. For example, Arwen sent the message in Figure 4.4 to his partner, which then formed the basis of subsequent exchanges about lifestyles and interests.

p.s please reaply to my? (this means questions)
do u like fairy tales?
are u into furry suff?

Figure 4.4 Arwen's soft toy and email text

The children then worked with their partners to develop an electronic presentation that could be delivered to student teachers. The aims of this presentation were to inform the audience of the interests, culture and lifestyle of young children. At this stage, the children developed multimodal texts that incorporated their own images, cartoons, clip art and photographs from the web (see Figures 4.5, 4.6 and 4.7).

SPECIAL PEOPLE

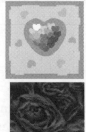

LOVE COMES NATURALLY TO SOME
PEOPLE AND WHICH IS TRUE LOVE.
IF A BOY IS IN LOVE WITH A GIRL HE
HAS A CRUSH ON HER AND HE MAY
CALL HER HIS GIRLFRIEND. AND
VISA VERSA WITH A GIRL.

Figure 4.5 Extract from presentation (1)

SPECIAL THINGS

The dream catcher has come from Majorca from my nan.

Figure 4.6 Extract from presentation (2)

As we all now that when a new member joins the family it brings joy and love to the family, so be full of happiness if you have a baby brother or sister.

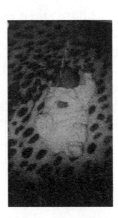

Figure 4.7 Extract from presentation (3)

The process of developing the presentations was complex, given the children's divergent interests, but eventually they were completed both virtually, via email, and through two face-to-face meetings that proved to be an important element of planning. The final presentations were varied, but all reflected something of the vibrant interests of this group of children, as the extract from one of them indicates (see Figure 4.8).

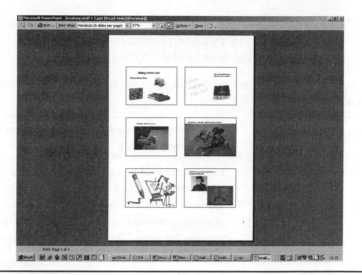

Figure 4.8 Making stuff is cool

There is no space within this chapter to review the range of learning that occurred in this project, nor can we discuss in any depth the implications of this work in terms of new textual practices. For this analysis, we refer you to the paper written by the project team (Burnett et al., 2004). The project enabled children to engage in a range of social practices in which aspects of their out-of-school life were valued and allowed them to use the technologies available to them to develop multimodal texts for a specific purpose.

Once their presentations were completed, the children presented their work to a group of student teachers at the university. Malden was amazed by the confidence children demonstrated in doing this. She had deliberately chosen children to get involved who were rather more reticent than the rest of the class, as she felt the project might develop their self-esteem, and the presentation of their work to a group of adult strangers would have been inconceivable to her at the start of the project.

The project team, along with the teachers involved, felt that the project had been a great success:

> We suggest that e-mail partnerships are worthwhile because they provide experience of an important medium of asynchronous communication. Furthermore, they can help to dissolve the walls of the classroom, and provide new purposes and audiences for children's writing. They also provide opportunity for early exploration of two key characteristic of new media – interactivity and multimodality. (Burnett et al., 2004: 16)

Returning to Lankshear and Knobel's (2004a) four principles of learning, it can be seen that Malden's practice can be mapped against the principles

(Table 4.4), which suggests that an element of this project's success was the way in which it was underpinned by sensitivity to aspects of 'imode pedagogy' (Lankshear and Knobel, 2004a).

Table 4.4 Malden's practice in relation to Lankshear and Knobel's (2004a) four principles of learning

Principle	Description (from Lankshear and Knobel, 2004a)	Malden's practice
The principle of efficacious learning	Learning should be connected in meaningful ways to learners' social and cultural practices. Learning should be inseparable from Discourses (Gee 1996).	Malden provided curriculum opportunities that were linked to children's understanding of email and e-communicative practices outside of school.
The principle of integrated learning	Integrated learning is situated inside a practice and relates to our identities. Learning is holistic and organic; it does not consist of learning 'chunks' in isolation from the Discourse as a whole.	Children learned about how to construct electronic texts in an integrated manner. The email communication was undertaken for the purpose of developing an understanding of each other's identities. Children then learned how to develop an electronic presentation on identities. This was for the purpose of presenting the work to an external audience.
The principle of productive appropriation and extension in learning	The process of learning should not involve conflict between social identities. Learning should provide opportunities for learners to transfer specific discursive practices into new spaces.	Children were able to transfer their knowledge of electronic texts experienced out-of-school to this activity.
The principle of critical learning	Learners should experience different and competing Discourses and be able to navigate critically these contested spaces.	Children were able to navigate a range of texts in a critical manner, deciding which texts to adopt and integrate into their own and which to reject. They were also aware of tensions between wanting to make the presentations meaningful to their own peer group and to the external (adult) audience.

Although this case study has featured the involvement of researchers from a local university, it does not present an outline of practice requiring this kind of involvement; it could be developed by a teacher in touch with staff in a partner school. However, the partnership of teachers with mentors/collaborators from higher education institutions is a strong model that has led to much exciting research in recent years (Nixon and Comber, 2005).

Malden's literacy curriculum is built on recognition of the skills the children bring with them to school as a result of engagement with technology outside the classroom. Many of them, Malden suggests, use mobile phones and email software on a regular basis in the home. In addition, children are competent in a wide range of technologies from a very young age (Marsh, 2004b; forthcoming; Rideout et al., 2003). This competence is rarely acknowledged or built upon effectively within classroom contexts (Lankshear and Knobel, 2003a). Malden recognizes that literacy is changing as a result of technological advances and she plans her curriculum in order to build on children's new media-related literacy practices.

In addition, Malden understands that the nature of the authoring process is changing in relation to new technologies. Despite Malden's lack of potentially useful resources, such as laptops for each child or tablet personal computers (PCs), she manages to forge a literacy curriculum which acknowledges the way literacy is being transformed in a highly technologized society. The children in her class develop a large range of skills, knowledge and understanding in relation to a variety of hardware and software, and also have opportunities to create and respond to multimodal texts.

Malden and Merchant's ongoing work contributes to the limited literature we have with regard to new technologies, literacy and primary schooling. Lankshear and Knobel (2003a; 2004a) have outlined a project in Australia entitled 'Knowledge Producing Schools' (Bigum, 2002), in which pupils create meaningful, authentic multimodal texts that arise from real-life problems children themselves have identified. This is exciting work that offers new models of learning. However, such work needs to be embedded in wider educational practice and this has major implications for the way in which we approach educational change. In the final part of this chapter, we present an interview with Michele Knobel and Colin Lankshear, who reflect on some of these complex issues.

INTERVIEW WITH MICHELE KNOBEL AND COLIN LANKSHEAR

WHAT ASPECTS OF THIS CASE STUDY DO YOU THINK REFLECT THE MAIN TENETS OF CURRENT THINKING ABOUT TEACHING AND LEARNING LITERACY IN A NEW MEDIA AGE?

Perhaps the first thing we should recognize here is that 'current thinking about teaching and learning literacy in a new media age' is extremely diverse and deeply divided. There is not just one 'current' of thought. In some of our work together and with other people we have identified two very different competing mindsets within current thinking about the world generally in relation to new technologies (Lankshear and Bigum, 1999; Lankshear and Knobel, 2003a; see also Barlow, in Tunbridge, 1995). One mindset approaches the world as though it is much the same as it has been in the past, only now it is a little more 'technologized'. People operating from this mindset apply familiar concepts, beliefs, strategies, and so on, to dealing with new technologies within everyday practices – including educational practices. They try to 'accommodate' new technologies to the world they already know and to ways they are familiar with that belong to this world. At the simplest level, this involves things like thinking of a word processor as a kind of typewriter, or of a computer as like a television. Elsewhere it shows up in things like trying to 'censor' use of the Internet by applying logics that apply to 'physical spaces' – such as using blocks and filters and similar forms of 'security'. In education it often shows up as using new technologies to do familiar things – for example, using PowerPoint or web pages to (re)tell narratives. It also shows up in things like talking about 'plagiarism' and 'critical evaluation' in relation to online texts in the same ways that we have talked about them in relation to printed texts. Of course, education policy and curriculum 'development' are saturated in this first mindset. Even when this is not the default mode for individual teachers and teacher educators, they quickly encounter it when faced with the task of 'using computers' to promote 'national curriculum objectives', in accordance with specified 'outcomes standards', while ensuring 'safety and security' on 'the information superhighway'.

The other mindset approaches the world as though it is very different from how it was in the past, and as though this difference has a lot to do with the emergence and subsequent development of new technologies. This mindset recognizes or accepts that new technologies have been integral to a global process of radical change. From this mindset, the role of new technologies in classrooms is not at all to preserve familiar practices and routines or even to 'add' new technologies to them. Rather, it is to radically reconfigure *what* is to be learned and *how* it is to be learned, including the role and place of new technologies themselves within such learning. It is important to recognize here that in places like North America, many European countries, Australasia and the like, we now have entire generations who have no personal experience of 'the world before computers'. They thus may have acquired this second mindset 'free' and be quite bemused by thinking and practices based on the other mindset. For such 'insiders' using the Internet, for instance, might be much more about communicating and exploring identities, text jamming, and moving memes around, than about, say, observing correct grammatical and spelling conventions, reproducing face-to-face kinds of interactions, and locating 'true' information.

Something of what is at stake between these two mindsets is evident in what Percirion (his online alias) has to say during data collection for an online ethnography of Internet chat spaces (Thomas, 2004; 2005). Percirion began participating regularly in online interaction spaces when he was 7 years old and was 14 when interviewed by Thomas ('Anya').

> *Anya: So what computer skills / knowledge are you getting at your school perc?*

> *President Percirion (UFP): Typing ...*
> *President Percirion (UFP): I'm a 42-words-per-min typer*
> *President Percirion (UFP): How to Use the Internet*
> *President Percirion (UFP): How Not To Use the Internet ...*
> *[...]*
> *President Percirion (UFP): And we're also learning how to use various computer systems*
> *President Percirion (UFP): Which I am sure will be out of date by the time we leave*
> *Anya: What various computer systems?*
> *President Percirion (UFP): Excel, Word, More Excel, Office*
> *President Percirion (UFP): PowerPoint ...*

On another occasion Percirion tells Thomas that what he has learned about relationships in his own time online helps him greatly in his offline life, and compares this to his school experience of 'ICT':

> *online, people come, go ... there's a whole world of people to talk to, you need to learn tolerance. It's the community and the people that kids can interact with that's really teaching them a lot about the social world. But*

> *maybe this is just my irritation with what schools do coming through – I mean schools claim to be teaching ICT (a term I hate) but they only do the 'I' (information) and always seem to neglect the 'C' (communication).*

Against this background we can discern elements of both mindsets in the case study. In relation to the second mindset, the teacher and researcher are keenly aware of the need to avoid the 'old wine in new bottles' syndrome as far as possible. This is reflected in the emphasis given in the project to engaging in identity work through online communication. It is also reflected in the ways the new technologies were used to mediate *relationships* between participants that move well beyond all too common teacher-mandated 'keypal' email exchanges between students.

Following Michael Schrage (1998; 2000), Chris Bigum (2002: 135) reminds us that 'the biggest impact digital technologies are having and will continue to have is on relationships between people and relationships between people and organisations'. Schrage (1997) argues that we often think of new technologies and, particularly, the Internet, in terms of an information design sensibility. (A 'design sensibility' is a bias or a skew in how we think about a new technology.) That is, we think of new technologies as being mainly about locating, obtaining, producing, exchanging and receiving information. This, of course, is precisely what Percirion observes about ICT in school. Operating from an information design sensibility is highly limited (and limiting) and actually flies in the face of facts. Mixing humour and insight, Schrage (2000: np) suggests that to say 'the Internet is about "information" is a bit like saying that "cooking" is about oven temperatures; it's technically accurate, but fundamentally untrue'. To the extent that the project was based on 'relationship work' the case study reflects the kind of thinking we associate with the second mindset. The world of relationships between individuals and between individuals and organizations has changed, and continues to change, profoundly, with the escalation and evolution of digital technology uses.

WHAT DO YOU SEE AS THE MOST IMPORTANT CONTRIBUTION RESEARCHING TECHNO-LITERACY PRACTICES CAN MAKE TO CLASSROOM PRACTICE?

This is an interesting question that raises what has become for us a serious issue. We think the most important contribution such research can make is *indirect*. Research that provides rich accounts of new social practices mediated by new technologies and multimodal texts can help inform teachers and others involved in education about what the world is like beyond the school gates. And the more such knowledge and understanding educators have, the better position they are in to judge how best to integrate (or not) new technologies into school work. During the 1990s we read everything we could get our hands on that offered insider accounts of cybercultures. These were mainly *not* texts written by academics or by people who would regard themselves as (highbrow) *researchers* of *technoliteracies*. They were accessible, 'down home' descriptions of people's experiences in multiuser dungeons (MUDs) and multiuser object-orientations (MOOs), in Silicon Valley start-up companies, of hackers and great hacks, of inventors and innovators, of programmers and sysops (system operators) and bulletin board hosts, of geeks, and so on. We lost ourselves in the wonder, mystery and sheer magic of how strings of 0s and 1s could produce sound, colour and movement in conjunction with magnets and lasers. We read it simply because it was interesting, and in the process we learned things we regard as among the most important and valuable things we have ever learned. And we read almost *none* of it with a view to thinking about how we could apply it in our lives. We just wanted to know.

Every day, in all kinds of ways, this knowledge helps us in our work and other aspects of our lives. This is rarely, however, in direct, functional, *applied* ways. It is more in terms of providing us with concepts and examples developed by 'insiders' that help us make sense of things we see and read about, or that provide clues about what to look out for in the way of trends and changes, and where to go to find out what is going on. We still have to do the interpretive work and 'nut out' specific applications. But we have a 'worldview' and a bit of a 'knowledge base' from which to do this.

We think that this is how research can work best to contribute to classroom practice: to make available to educators rich examples and useful concepts they can draw on in working out how to 'do' good pedagogy. We would like to see a moratorium on research that 'delivers' activities and modules and professional development 'tricks' designed for classroom application. In place of this we would prefer to see research that provides rich and theorized accounts of cultural practices that enable and encourage educators to experience them from the inside, as participants. From this basis teachers are in an optimal position to make productive connections between learners' prior knowledge and experiences, the potential of new technologies to expand student learning, their own knowledge and theory relevant to teaching and learning, and the learning goals and outcomes to which they are committed.

WHAT IDEAS DO YOU HAVE FOR HELPING TEACHERS TO UNDERSTAND AND IMPLEMENT THE KINDS OF PRINCIPLES YOU ADVANCE FOR I-MODE PEDAGOGY?

In our paper about planning pedagogy for i-mode we try to anticipate the introduction of wireless Internet into schools and to suggest principles that might guide the use of wireless technologies and applications like mobile phones and wireless or Bluetooth personal digital assistant (PDAs) in conjunction with other highly mobile technologies, like digital recorders, iPods and other mobile multimedia players, and digital cameras. We gave the example of teams of students, teachers and academics using a range of such technologies to undertake an oral history project with migrant families who had lived in the community for a long time. We described how students could use mobile phones to 'report in' from the field (out in the community) as they collected interview and artifact data, and how they could use a wireless 'hotspot' in a community space to send files to the project website and weblog using a PDA or Notebook to which they had previously uploaded digital voice recordings, photos, and the like. Our principles included very simple things like the principle of providing space for young people to use technologies and applications they are familiar with from other spaces in their lives for purposes related to school-based learning. So an iPod that doubles as a hard disk and a voice recorder, but that learners may use mainly for downloading and playing music and sharing music files with peers, can easily become a research tool. The same is true for mobile phones that have built-in cameras and are Internet capable.

We think that the best way for teachers to understand and implement a principle like finding ways of building tools and processes with which young people are familiar and comfortable within other contexts into formal learning contexts is to have some personal experience with the tools themselves, some experience with social practices in which they are used and which count as bona fide learning contexts (for example, doing an oral history research project), and some general knowledge of digitally mediated worlds of the kind described in our response to the previous question. The point about having direct and indirect experience of new technologies grounded in 'mature' versions of social practices (Gee et al., 1996: ch. 1) cannot be overemphasized. This is the surest guide to meeting the principle of efficacious learning (which refers to engaging students in learning *now* that is related in motivated and meaningful ways to things learners will do and be at *further* points in their life trajectories). In contexts where participants in social practices are actively looking for ways to improve the practice, to innovate and to become better at what they do, it is also one of the best bases for understanding and implementing the principle of critical learning. Possibly the best way of making the point, however, is by referring to a text like Jim Gee's (2003) *What Video Games Have to Teach Us about Learning and Literacy*. In each of his six chapters about different kinds of computing and video games, Gee identifies six principles for learning (making 36 principles in all). While we may gain some understanding of these chapters just by reading the book, the best way to understand them is by replicating the process out of which Gee framed the principles: by playing the games that embody them.

This is why we are such strong advocates of the fledgling Knowledge Producing Schools (KPS) initiative (see Bigum, 2002; Lankshear and Knobel, 2003a: 105–8; Lankshear and Knobel 2004a). 'Doing pedagogy' in KPS projects is built on developing new and interesting relationships with groups in their local communities, by engaging in processes that generate truly useful products or performances that are valued by the 'clienteles' for whom they have been produced. An important part of negotiating the production of such knowledge is that the product or performance is something that students see as being valued by the consumer or audience of their work and is evaluated using the same criteria applied to evaluating adult-produced products and performances. The students know their work is taken seriously, and that it has to be good or else it will not be acceptable to those who have commissioned it. The level of engagement and the quality of work and student learning to date have been impressive.

The examples that follow are not teacher-centered projects with peripheral student involvement. Rather, they are projects – in the sense in which the task of developing and producing a commercial movie or a new motor car are often called 'projects' – that are sometimes presented to students as problems to solve or, as has frequently been the case, problems the students have raised themselves with a view to solving them. For example:

- Groups of Grade 6 students worked in collaboration with the local cattle sale yards to produce a documentary on the history of the sale yards for a Beef Exposition in 2003. They video-interviewed representatives of different sectors in the cattle industry, recorded *in situ* footage of activities, provided voice-overs and bridges between sequences, and so on, and edited the components to produce the documentary as a CD. The product CD is being used at an international beef exposition and by the local council to promote the region.

■ A group of students interviewed and filmed local 'characters' at tourist sites in an old mining town with high unemployment rates and that is trying to establish itself as a tourist location. The students shot the film, edited it, and burned the product to CD. This product can now be accessed at various sites around the town via touch screen computers so visitors can get a sense of what the town has to offer (cf. Bigum, 2003: 5–6).

WHAT IMPLICATIONS MIGHT THESE IDEAS HAVE FOR FURTHER RESEARCH?

There are many possible implications, but we have space to mention just two or three briefly. First, we think education can only benefit from a lot more research of the kind being done by people like Angela Thomas (2004; 2005), Kevin Leander and colleagues (Leander, 2003; Leander and McKim, 2003) and James Paul Gee (2003). This is pure basic research of authentic social practices, with little or no pretence to distill functional classroom applications. It is research that is rich in description and rigorous in its attempts to understand and interpret what is going on from the inside of the practices being observed and to avoid as far as possible crunching data through preset concepts and explanations.

Second, we think education can only benefit from a reduction in applied research – and, particularly, contract research – that aims to provide pedagogical 'quick fixes', 'off the shelf modules' and 'professional development packages' that divert teachers from the hard work required to develop good pedagogy.

Finally, we think teachers should be encouraged to engage in research of digitally mediated social practices in contexts beyond classrooms. We do not believe that teacher research has to involve teachers researching their own or other people's classrooms (Lankshear and Knobel, 2004b). Indeed, we think teachers could do little better than to undertake the kinds of research represented by Thomas, Leander, Gee and others like them.

CONCLUSION

In this chapter, we have considered aspects of curricula and pedagogy in a new media age. The theoretical framework introduced was one in which, in an era of swift technological advancement, the nature of literacy has been subject to interrogation and uncertainty. Amongst this epistemological and ontological anxiety, the work of a number of educators has sought to explore the opportunities and challenges presented by these changes. The case study illustrated aspects of a pedagogy that embraced new technologies, and the interview with Knobel and Lankshear further developed understanding of the way in which classrooms can become innovative and challenging spaces where 'insider' knowledge is valued and extended in critical ways. In the next chapter, we move on to consider the nature of sociocultural historical theory and focus on the potential for classrooms to foster productive communities of practice.

NOTES

1   For examples of use of innovative technologies, see the Nesta Futurelab website at http://www.nestafuturelab.org/showcase/show.htm.

CHAPTER 5

Sociocultural-Historical Theory

Humans develop through their changing participation in the sociocultural
activities of their communities, which also change. (Rogoff, 2003: 11)

What does it mean to say that learning is changing participation? What role
does change play in learning? How do activities change by our participation in them? And what does any of this have to do with classrooms? It has
always been surprising to us that people talk about teaching yet tend not to
talk about learning. When people do talk about learning they usually
assume a shared understanding of what learning means and how people
do it. It is commonly based on their own perceptions of how they learned
and that 'real' learning, whatever that means, happens in school. Recent
scholarship in literacy has challenged both traditional and current assumptions about learning and where it occurs (Gee, 2003; in press; Hull and
Schultz, 2002; Larson, 2005; Street, 2005). In this chapter, we draw on
research in cultural psychology to outline what Rogoff (2003) has called
sociocultural-historical theory and connect that theory to research, scholarship and practice in literacy.

THEORETICAL FOCUS

Sociocultural-historical learning theory defines the child as an active member
of a constantly changing community of learners in which knowledge constructs and is constructed by larger cultural systems (Cole, 1996; Lee and
Smagorinsky, 2000; Rogoff, 2003). Explanations of the active nature of the
learning process often refer to knowledge construction as being mutually con-

stituted. Cole links the term 'constituted' to intention: 'The dual process of shaping and being shaped through culture implies that humans inhabit "intentional" (constituted) worlds within which the traditional dichotomies of subject and object, person and environment, and so on, cannot be analytically separated and temporally ordered into independent and dependent variables' (1996: 103). We can link the idea of intention, or the constitution, of knowledge (literacy knowledge in particular) to the dynamic learning processes that occur in classrooms which are grounded in sociocultural-historical theory. Mutuality is an inevitable process that emerges when humans interact to learn, hence knowledge as a mutually constituted social, cultural and historical process. What is interesting about this perspective is that it steps outside traditional dichotomies that teachers tend not to rethink (for example, subject/object, or student/literacy). In rethinking these relationships as dynamically co-constructed by both teachers and students, we can begin to see how contexts for learning can be reconstructed to enable the fundamentally social and cultural processes of learning discussed in this framework.[1]

Sociocultural-historical theory presents a culturally focused analysis of participation in everyday life, in both formal and informal learning settings, that offers teachers and researchers a way to meaningfully use or analyze students' practices in the classroom or research project. In this view, literacy is a tool for interpreting what people from different communities do, not simply what they do not do when compared to a dominant group. Rogoff puts it this way:

> *Interpreting the activity of people without regard for* their *meaning system and goals renders observations meaningless. We need to understand the coherence of what people from different communities* do, *rather than simply determining that some other group of people do* not *do what 'we' do, or do not do it as well or in the way that we do it, or jumping to conclusions that their practices are barbaric. (2003: 17, emphases in original)*

This perspective of learning and culture helps teachers to see how children 'live culturally' (Moll, 2000) rather than isolating culture from the practice of everyday life and highlights students' practices as valuable resources for curriculum. Furthermore, conceptualizing learning from this perspective constitutes a shift from traditional teacher-centered or student-centered classrooms (concepts familiar to most teachers) to conceiving of classrooms as learning-centered contexts for learning. Rogoff et al. (2001) have articulated how teachers might conceptualize and make use of such a shift when designing, implementing and assessing curricula.

SOCIAL ORIGINS OF LEARNING

According to Cole (1996), human thought processes are fundamentally social in origin and develop through the following key processes: cultural mediation, historical development and practical activity. *Cultural mediation* refers to how humans modify mental and material objects (tool, artifacts) to regulate interaction with the world and with others. Language and literacy are key mediating artifacts for meaning construction, for example. *Historical development* is a process in which humans arrange for the use of existing tools over time, although as Rogoff (2003) argues, those tools are transformed by each generation of use. *Practical activity* claims that human psychological functions are grounded in everyday activities and practices. Cole states the connection of these ideas to education:

> *This view of social origins requires paying special attention to adults' power to arrange children's environments so as to optimize their development according to existing norms. It generates the idea of a 'zone of proximal development' which affords the proximal, relevant environment of experience for development. It is the foundation upon which, in an ideal world, the education of children would be organized. (1996: 111)*

What are the implications for organizing literacy learning from this perspective? If learning is a mutually constituted social, cultural and historical process that is mediated by language and interaction, then the context (both material and social) needs to foster this process. We would expect table groupings rather than rows, for example, and more time for small-group or paired interaction so that children and adults can use the cultural tools for thinking they bring to the classroom. In other words, children are key in constructing the learning; children are not 'constructed' in some linear way by teachers (Rogoff et al., 2001).

Children use the tools for thinking, such as literacy, through interaction with more skilled partners (adults and/or peers) within the *zone of proximal development* (Vygotsky, 1962; 1978). As Rogoff argues 'Artifacts such as books, orthographies, computers, languages, and hammers are essentially social, historical objects, transforming with the ideas of both their designers and their later users. They form and are formed by the practices of their use and by related practices, in historical and anticipated communities' (2003: 276). This suggests that literacy knowledge is constructed through tools teachers and students use in everyday life, in and out of school (such as traditional texts, multimodal textual practices such as instant messaging or blogging, that is, online web diaries, and computers)

Teachers can use this framework to better understand how literacy learning happens in their classrooms and beyond and how to use their students' 'linguistic and cultural-historical repertoires' (Gutierrez and Rogoff, 2003: 22) as curricular resources. Furthermore, this framework helps to break the hegemony of the deficit model (Gutierrez and Rogoff, 2003; James-Wilson, 2004; Larson and Irvine, 1999; Rogoff, 2003; Woods, 2004) by conceiving of literacy as a social practice that looks at what people *do* with literacy in their everyday lives and by actively using those practices in the classroom (Ball, 1995; Lee, 2001). Building on Moll (2000), teachers and researchers alike can ask how their students (or research participants) live literately and for what purposes? In this chapter, we draw on Rogoff's recent (2003) work to outline a definition of learning as changing participation and use this framework to describe the classroom applications of sociocultural-historical theory in our case study.

Before we go too much further, however, we should go back to the 'beginning', so to speak. The next section briefly outlines the roots of current thinking in this framework.[2] We close the chapter with an interview with Barbara Rogoff after illustrating the theory in a classroom case example.

HISTORICAL GROUND

What to call a theory of learning based on the work of Vygotsky has gone through its own evolution (for example, sociocultural, cultural-historical) that is related to the goals and purposes of scholars (Lee and Smagorinsky, 2000) and has evolved out of studies of practice (Cole and Engeström, 1993; Moll, 1990). It is at base a theory of human development. Historically, education has relied on traditional psychology to explain learning and development. Theories rooted in educational psychology suggest that development is based on maturation and seek to establish developmental norms in research. In this traditional perspective, instruction should follow development and to introduce learning activities before a child is mature enough would result in failure (Elkind, 1981; Gesell, 1940).

Research on development in early childhood that was based on Piaget (1926), and influenced by the maturationist view, introduced the notion that children constructed knowledge from their experiences across a sequence of stages. How they constructed this knowledge and what knowledge was constructed were determined by their developmental level, not necessarily their age (Rogoff, 2003). Learning was defined as an individual process of growth through progressive stages of cognitive development. In this view of learning, teachers designed curricula that coincided with a child's developmental level in order to be 'developmentally appropriate' (Bredekamp, 1987). While some of this research acknowledges the socio-cultural processes involved in learning, the primary focus is on individual growth and development, and is based on the premise that instruction follows development (Saracho and Spodek, 1993).

VYGOTSKY'S CONTRIBUTION

The work of Vygotsky (1962; 1978) has transformed our understanding of learning in early childhood, and language and literacy learning in particular. Vygotsky (1962) offers a detailed, comprehensive analysis of the relationship between thought and speech, and argues that the primary function of speech is communication or social interaction. Vygotsky's analysis is through units (thought and speech interrelated and mutually constituted) that retain all the basic properties of the whole. Vygotsky uses the classic example of water (H_2O). He argues that we cannot understand the meaning of water by separating it into its component parts (for example, hydrogen and oxygen). Hydrogen is hydrogen and oxygen is oxygen. It is only when they are brought together in a particular way that we get what we understand as 'water'. What we do with water varies by culture and history, and thus the meaning of water varies. Edelsky (1991) connects this idea to literacy learning with her bike-riding metaphor. We do not learn to ride a bike by first learning peddling, steering and balancing. We learn to ride a bike by riding a bike with the help of someone who knows how. How people ride bikes and for what purposes varies, but learning to bike-ride is still constructed in interaction. In other words, people learn to read by reading and to write by writing, with the assistance of an expert or more proficient other, about something and for a specific purpose or purposes.

To connect this idea more closely to literacy, we come to understand that word meaning exists in a dynamic relationship between thought and language in interaction as literacy knowledge is mutually constituted. Vygotsky (1978) argues that all thought occurs first in social interaction on the interpsychological plane, and then gradually moves to the internal or intrapsychological plane as the child appropriates knowledge. Furthermore, the concept of literacy learning as interactional connects to Gee's (1996) conception of D/discourse described in Chapter 1 by understanding language as a mediating tool in the construction of identity, social languages (Bakhtin, 1981) and community languages (Lee and Smagorinsky, 2000) that serve as resources used both deliberately and implicitly by students and teachers in the co-construction of literacy knowledge.

Most notably, Vygotsky introduced the notion that learning can occur before development in what he (1962; 1978) termed the *zone of proximal development*. The zone of proximal development (sometimes referred to as 'zoped' or 'zpd') represents the range of a child's ability characterized by the discrepancy between a child's current level and the level of ability she reaches in solving problems with assistance. This conception of learning situates an individual within the concrete social context of learning and development and provides a unit of study that integrates the individual with the social environment (Moll, 1990). Designing activities that promote learning just beyond the child's developmental level, then providing assistance or scaffolding (Bruner, 1975) during the activity, serves to extend development (Saracho and Spodek, 1993) and move the child through his/her zone. The zone shifts forward and new challenging activities can be presented that draw on the child's previous experiences. From this perspective, then, instruction precedes development.

IMPLICATIONS FOR CLASSROOMS

The work undertaken in relation to sociocultural-historical theory has a number of important implications for curriculum and pedagogy. In the following sections, we reflect on the notion of learning as changing participation, introduced in Chapter 1, the role of community in classrooms and the nature of learning on multiple planes.

LEARNING AS CHANGING PARTICIPATION

This view of learning has influenced current research on literacy learning and has become familiar to some teachers through professional reading or education conferences. The concept of emergent literacy, for example, addresses the range of ability now understood as part of children's development of literacy competence over time. Emergent literacy suggests that children learn as they are engaged in language activities that are preparatory to learning to write in more formal settings (Saracho and Spodek, 1993). This view of literacy learning represents a shift from a readiness perspective that emphasized the mastery of discrete skills to the understanding that children develop a set of behaviors and concepts about literacy that precede the development of conventional literacy skills (Sulzby, 1989).

Learning occurs, therefore, through participation in social, cultural and historical contexts that are mediated by interaction. Thus children learn by participating in sociocultural activity, in both formal and informal contexts. Specifically, children learn the meaning of written language in the context of culturally relevant situations (Daiute, 1993; Lee, 2001) both in and out of school. In this view, the focus is not on transferring literacy knowledge from those who know more to those who know less but on the collaborative use of mediational means, such as literacy, to construct and communicate meaning (Moll, 1990). This notion of the co-construction of literacy learning reflects the critical consciousness of problem-posing education that unveils reality for both student and teacher, and acknowledges the children as possessing the literate voice we discussed in Chapter 3 (Freire, 1989). Children's capabilities as literate beings are recognized and legitimized in the classroom and the community.

THE ROLE OF COMMUNITY

'Community' is a term thrown around a lot in education these days. What does it mean to say 'classroom community' or 'community of learners'? Teachers are expected to construct a 'community' in their classrooms year after year with different children and their families. How does this happen? What does community mean? From a sociocultural-historical perspective, community is expanded to include the larger society as a community of practice or, multiple communities of practice, to which children are being socialized on multiple levels. Think of what might be a typical day for children of primary school age on a school day in the West. They get up, eat breakfast, and leave for school (walking, riding a bus, or getting a ride from a parent or caregiver). At home they may have watched television, listened to music, and completed homework. Crossing from home (private) to community, then school (public) spaces, the child walks through a host of communities of practice (bus drivers, walkers, riders, carpool). Both at home and in school, they participate in multiple communities simultaneously. They are students, children and learners participating in a community of teachers, adults, parents and professionals, each with its own set of practices and discourses.

Lave and Wenger define community of practice as a 'set of relations among persons, activity, and world over time and in relation with other tangential and overlapping communities of practice' (1991: 98). Learning occurs through participation in social practices, such as schooling for example, that are motivated by the desire to become full participants in communities of practice. Lee and Smagorinsky describe community as being more than a 'sense of harmony, but rather to a shared set of social practices and goals that become differentiated among subgroups' (2000: 5). Rogoff et al. describe community as involving:

relationships among people based on common endeavors – trying to accomplish some things together – with some stability of involvement and attention to the ways that members relate to each other. In other words, a community of learners develops 'cultural' practices and traditions that transcend the particular individuals involved, such as expected ways of handling conflicts and interpersonal issues and crises, as well as traditions for celebrating turning points and successes. (2001: 10)

If we look at classrooms as culturally embedded communities of learners that are reflective of and creators of social hierarchies in the larger society, then we can determine how and in what ways students are socialized to become competent members of their communities, multiple communities, and perhaps, how and to what degree they are differentially socialized. Children are necessarily legitimate peripheral participants in adult social worlds or communities of practice as they go about their daily activities (Lave and Wenger, 1991). In many white middle-class households in the USA or the UK, for example, children participate in family activities such as grocery shopping and meal preparation, but are separated from most adult activities. In many other communities, children participate broadly in the full range of community activities (Heath, 1983; Rogoff, 1990; 2003).

Furthermore, as Rogoff explains, 'communities can be defined as groups of people who have some common and continuing organization, values, understanding, history, and practices' (2003: 80). She goes on to explain how community:

- requires structured communication that is expected to endure for some time, with a degree of commitment and shared through often contested meaning and discourses;[3]

- develops cultural practices and traditions that transcend the particular individuals involved, as one generation replaces another;

- involves generations that move through it, with customary ways of handling the transitions of generations.

The challenge for teachers is to build and maintain a meaningful learning community, a community of learners in the short time frame of an academic year, whilst facing increasing scrutiny from governments and the general public.

▓ PARTICIPATION ON MULTIPLE PLANES

Rogoff (1992) helps to clarify the layered complexity of participating in multiple communities by thinking about participation as occurring on three, mutually constituted planes: (1) apprenticeship, (2) guided participation and (3) participatory appropriation. *Apprenticeship* corresponds to the plane of community activity in which caregivers, or teachers, in the case of schools, arrange the occurrence of children's activities and facilitate learning by regulating the difficulty of the tasks and by modeling expert performance during joint participation in activity. *Guided participation* refers to interpersonal processes occurring in everyday activity. Guided participation co-ordinates the adult's attempt to orient the children to the task, to provide links between current knowledge and the knowledge to be appropriated, and to structure the activity so as to afford the children a range of choices that can guide decision-making, with their roles collaboratively adjusted so that they are involved at a level that is challenging but within reach (for example, within their zone of proximal development). Guided participation also uses culturally constructed and valued tools and/or signs in this co-constructed process of literacy learning. *Participatory appropriation* corresponds to personal processes in which the individual changes through participation in activity and indicates how that participation prepares the individual for future similar activities. Rogoff emphasizes the routine, often tacit, nature of participation in culturally organized activity to point to observing change in a community of learners.

Guided participation emerges as key for applying sociocultural-historical theory to classrooms. The principles of guided participation are present in multiple contexts, in and out of school, but can be particularly useful for teachers when teaching literacy so they can move beyond simply correcting papers, and think instead about what specific instructional strategies, or scaffolds, students need to compose (revise, edit, publish) a variety of texts. This might include multimodal, post-typographic texts, such as a website or blog (Lankshear and Knobel, 2003b). Teachers can orient students to tasks by saying 'Tell me about your story' or asking questions such as 'What sounds do you hear?' when young children ask how to spell a word, as the teacher in our case study classroom does, or questions/activities needed for constructing/using websites that do not just put 'new wine in an old bottle' (Lankshear and Knobel, 2003a).

Building on Rogoff's (1994) articulation of a community of learners, we can put forward the following characteristics of a community of learners based on sociocultural-historical theory, as shown in Table 5.1.

Table 5.1 Characteristics of a community of learners

1. Learning is a social phenomenon mediated by language in interaction and by social and institutional processes as people accommodate each other's involvement both proximally (for example, guided participation) and distally (for example, class schedules, physical arrangement. See Rogoff et al., 2001, for further discussion).

2. Learning is defined as changing participation in culturally valued activity.

3. Learning is co-constructed through participation with others in routine everyday activity and social practices.

4. Development is described as changes in participants' responsibility rather than the presence or absence of participation (Griffin and Cole, 1984); students learn responsibility for their own actions and decisions (Rogoff, 1994).

5. The concept of the zone of proximal development offers an effective tool in the analysis and use of classroom interaction as a context for learning; the zoped, as opposed to what has been referred to as the next-step learning strategies seen in most classrooms (Griffin and Cole, 1984), includes multiple levels of a literacy task where a child is learning with support of adults and other experts on several levels of participation.

6. Both expert and novice are active members of the community; no role is passive by definition.

7. The curriculum focuses on the interests of the children and adults and provides opportunities for them to construct activity purposes (a focus on children's interests is not the same as student-centered) (Rogoff et al., 2001).

8. Instruction emphasizes process, not just finished products.

9. Collaborative learning occurs throughout the classroom, not just in isolated activities.

10. Adults serve as leaders and facilitators, however, leadership is shared; asymmetry of participation roles is inevitable.

11. Assessment occurs through ongoing observation and working with the child (for example, joint participation in activity); assessment informs instruction.

Our case study classroom will provide the context for seeing what these characteristics might look like in practice.[4]

IMPLICATIONS FOR RESEARCHING LITERACY

Understanding a form of life, or anyway some aspects of it to some degree, and convincing others that you have indeed done so, involves more than the assembly of telling particulars or the imposition of general narratives. It involves bringing figure and ground, the passing occasion and the long story, into coincident view. (Geertz, 1995: 51)

Research by advocates of cultural-historical and sociocultural approaches (Cole, 1996; Cole and Engeström, 1993; Gutierrez, 1993; 2002; Lave and Wenger, 1991; Lee and Smagorinsky, 2000; Moll, 1990; 2000; Rogoff, 1990; 1995; 2003; Scribner and Cole, 1981; Wertsch, 1991) situate learning in social structures, both formal and informal, in order to understand what gets learned, how it is learned, and with what variations and similarities (Gutierrez and Rogoff, 2003). Viewing literacy learning as socially situated expands our understanding of learning to include the social, cultural and historical contexts of an individual's existence. In this view, learning is inherently situated in social interactional, cultural, institutional and historical contexts, and constitutes the context for learning in which teachers and students construct authentic opportunities for learning (Putney et al., 2000).

The challenge for researchers is to describe whatever phenomenon is under study both locally and globally. On one hand, we need to offer as much detail as necessary to contribute to evidentiary warrant (Erickson, 1986). On the other hand, we need to present a broad enough discussion to be able to make some general statements. Sociocultural-historical theory helps researchers make more glocal (Kraidy, 1999) claims or arguments by focusing on activity goals across similar activities (for example, looking at how people do different things to accomplish similar goals) (Gutierrez and Rogoff, 2003; Rogoff, 2003).

Applying this idea to schools helps in the analysis of the multiple and often conflicting goals of schooling (Larson and Gatto, 2004). As Rogoff (2003: 34) states, 'a focus on the function (or purpose or goal) of people's behavior facilitates understanding of how different ways of doing things may be used to accomplish similar goals, or how similar ways of doing things may serve different goals'. Conflicting goals for schooling pose an interesting problem for researchers, not to mention the position in which it places teachers. For example, the goal of meaningful learning often runs in conflict with governmental legislation such as No Child Left Behind (NCLB) in the USA or the National Literacy Strategy in the UK. Understanding how teachers negotiate this tension for themselves, the curriculum and their students is an interesting research question that can be framed in sociocultural-historical theory.

CLASSROOM CASE STUDY: MARYRITA MAIER, GREECE CENTRAL SCHOOL DISTRICT, USA

It is hard not to recognize the quality of Maier's teaching once you see how this 28-year veteran teacher uses her more than 6,000 children's books and her own writing practices to teach 6- and 7-year-olds to write upwards of 45-page stories and chapter books and read books at a rate of 150 books per week (Larson and Maier, 2000). This section will use Maier's classroom as the case example of what sociocultural-historical theory (Rogoff, 2003) might look like in a classroom.

CONTEXT

Maryrita Maier has been a first grade teacher for her entire career. In fact, until 2002, she had taught first grade in the same school for over 25 years, long enough to be teaching children of children she taught when they were first graders. She made the decision to change districts and begin her tenure process all over again because pressure to conform to a phonics-only curriculum in her old district had become stifling. The district to which she transferred claimed to have a progressive, process-oriented program. As it turned out, the NCLB changed everything and the pressure to conform increased in every school. Like Lynn Gatto (see Chapter 2), she is currently pursuing her doctoral degree with Larson. The data used in this chapter comes from two sources: a year-long ethnography Larson conducted in Maier's room in 1996–97, and footage gathered while filming a documentary in her new classroom (Smith and Larson, 2004).

During the 1996–97 project described below (Larson and Maier, 2000), Maier taught in the only primary school (K-3) serving an isolated rural area. The building's windows looked out over the surrounding village landscape that included orchards, single-family homes and the village cemetery. There were approximately 600 students of mixed racial, ethnic and socio-economic backgrounds, most of whom were from working-class families in the surrounding neighborhood. Some students were from very poor working families or migrant families that came to the area for seasonal farm work. A few families lived in a small community of corporate executives near Lake Ontario. The year Larson observed, Maier had one student from the wealthy lakeside community, with the remainder coming from neighboring working-class families.

▦ PHYSICAL ENVIRONMENT AND RESOURCES

On first impression a visitor to Maier's classroom might feel claustrophobic: boxes and baskets of books occupied every open shelf and cupboard space, shelves were full of mathematics and science supplies, paper, writing tools of all kinds and colors, and more books. The room was brightly decorated with children's artwork, writing and literature-related theme bulletin boards. Much of the room decoration was typical of a first grade classroom in the USA (calendar, theme-related posters and bulletin boards, alphabet and number charts, and so on). The heart of the room was the carpet area where Maier modeled writing at the easel, read books aloud and generally conducted classroom business. There was no 'teacher' desk. She had two 'kidney'-shaped tables that she used for small-group work. The children's desks were arranged in groups of four, enabling rich interaction. Cubbies for coats, backpacks and boots in the winter, and the kitchen area, filled out the rest of the room.

Maier emphasized the development of community in her classroom from the first day of school. She explained that:

> you need to spend time with them. You need to – I eat lunch with them. I'm with them a lot. I make time for them. I write to them everyday. I know everything about their personal lives I could possibly know. I know the names of their dogs. I know the names of their family members. They know about my family. They know what I like to do. I know what they like to do and I think the familiarity of it helps. You can't have a sense of community if you don't have time, spend time.

Maier and her students stayed in the classroom to eat lunch together 'family style' rather than go to the noisy cafeteria. They knew each other's likes, dislikes and life passions intimately. In fact, they knew so much about Maier's husband that he would sometimes feel uncomfortable. He would arrive in the classroom to a flurry of questions about his mole problem in the garden, the family trip to New Hampshire or the play they had seen. He asked Maier, 'How do they know so much about me?' Maier always laughs when she thinks of her husband's face when the students start asking him these kinds of questions. Maier shares who she is with the students every day and this willingness to share her life and experiences with them through her writing and daily interactions builds trust. This trust in her and in their classmates makes it possible for students to write about their own lives, even painful events.

▨ THE CURRICULUM

Maier's literacy curriculum is founded on her belief in children as social learners. She designed a rich, engaging and relevant curriculum rooted in a passionate commitment to young children's literacy learning. She dedicates herself to investigating the most meaningful instructional tools for literacy, and then adapts them to align with what she knows to be the way children learn best. The end result is that the students who come through her room leave writing chapter books, having read hundreds of books from her collection and, most importantly, with a profound love of literacy and, of course, of 'Marvelous Mrs. Maier.'

A Day in the Life

A typical day in Maier's classroom began long before the children arrive at 8.30 in the morning. She was normally there early so that she had plenty of time to prepare for the students' arrival, or she would have stayed at school the night before until after 6 o'clock or sometimes later depending on whether there was a school event to attend. The first thing students did when they came in the morning was the book exchange. They would check in the books they took home the night before, and then select and check out a group of books for that night's reading. The book exchange was but one part of a complexly layered literacy curriculum and constituted the home reading program. Students took home a set of books every night in a zip-lock bag, read them, then brought them back the next morning.

After the exchange, students went to their desks to find the dialogue journal Maier had left for them. Each night, she wrote to her students and each morning they wrote back. She began this practice the first week of school and did it every day for the rest of the school year. Early on children read only the words they knew. The daily occurrence of this activity and the regular pattern of the text scaffolded their reading development over time. Maier always began with 'Dear' followed by the student's name. She wrote a sentence or two that ended in a question connected to what the student had written and signed off with 'love, Marvelous Mrs. Maier' (MMM for short), her nickname. Children picked up the opening and closings right away. To varying degrees they began to write back with parts of sentences, then full responses as their expertise emerged.

The rest of the morning consisted of an integrated mathematics, science, social studies and language arts curriculum that continued until lunch. Children were responsible for completing their work during this morning time period and for checking in with Maier before going outside. The class rule 'read to three then me' served to facilitate an interactive context in which students learned to work with each other in all classroom activities. When students were finished with their work, they invariably chose to read. They moved to the carpet area, pulled out a pile of books and read, both alone and with a group of friends. Maier always had a basket of Post-it notes available for students to write their names on and place in the inside cover of books. At the beginning of every year, each time she pulled out a book to read, she looks inside the front cover, finding the collection of Post-its left from the previous year's students. She excitedly exclaims, 'Look how much this book was loved! Now it's your turn'. From that moment on, students could not wait to put their own names on Post-its and place them inside all the books they read. By the end of the year, the books were filled with colorful Post-it notes with the names of all the children who read them.

KEY FEATURES OF PRACTICE

Describing Maier's literacy curriculum in detail would take its own book, so for this chapter we focus on several key activities: Morning Message and Writing Time; Read Aloud and Guided Reading. These activities will provide a context to discuss how Maier reconciles the increasingly constraining external mandates that reduce literacy to the so-called 'basics' with what she understands to be sound practice grounded in learning theory and literacy research. She does not separate skill from practices, for example. As in Edelsky's bike-riding metaphor, children learn to read by reading and to write by writing with someone who knows how.

The descriptions below were taken from observations conducted during filming for a documentary about teaching ways of coping with restrictive pedagogical mandates and from a professional development video (Smith and Larson, in production, 2004).

Morning Message
▬

Morning message satisfies many of the phonics and word work requirements of her district while, more importantly, setting the kids up for a day of learning. In Morning Message, Maier composes a message addressed to students that outlines the activities planned for the day. She writes about real upcoming activities for the class and the activity itself is her variation of a common activity in early childhood classrooms in the USA in which teachers write 'Today is Wednesday, yesterday was Tuesday and tomorrow is Thursday' as part of a calendar/schedule activity. She wrote this message on the chalkboard and addressed it like a letter (for example, 'Dear Students' to open and 'love, MMM' to close). The format mirrored the daily entries in the dialogue journals and served as another scaffold for students' changing participation in literacy learning. She read the message aloud as she wrote and students did their best to say the words along with her, predicting upcoming words to the best of their ability. The familiarity of the activities and its daily, routine presence made their reading fairly accurate, although she could always surprise them.

Phonics and word work requirements were met by what happened next. After the message was written and read aloud as a group, Maier began what she called 'word hunt'. Word hunt begins with a song and is followed by individual students coming up to the board and circling the word Maier asked students to find. For example, as a scaffold for students' understanding of consonant blends, she would ask, 'who can find all the "withs"?' or 'who can find what words that start with "th"?' Student volunteers came up to the board and circled the word, thereby finding the 'hunted' word. After word hunt, Maier shifted to another phase that focused more specifically on phonics. In this activity, Maier erased parts of words. Which parts she erased depended on her analysis of where the students were in terms of their learning needs. In other words, if her analysis of students' writing (for example, where they are in their zpd) showed that students were struggling with vowels or digraphs, she erased those parts in morning message. Some days she would erase consonant blends, other days it would be digraphs. She used an existing text with an authentic purpose as a meaningful context in which to scaffold students' learning school-based literacy skills.

Maier refers to her morning message activity as a 'humane' way to teach what is traditionally referred to as the basic skills of literacy. Morning Message is one example of how she teaches literacy conventions in the context of real text. While Maier limits her curriculum to school-based literacy practices, her practice does illustrate one way to meet external constraints humanly. Morning Message is real reading (writing), not a reading (writing) exercise (Edelsky, 1991). Most reading instruction in traditional classrooms uses reading exercises such a phonics worksheets or round-robin reading that is fundamentally not reading. The way Maier has constructed her literacy curriculum emphasizes the connection of reading and writing in the larger context of literacy and the social practices people have surrounding written text, while at the same time providing a context for explicit instruction of phonics, sentence construction, genre (specifically letter writing) and punctuation. Maier pulls from students' writing in designing her lessons on these parts of written language, selecting instructional strategies based on student needs. This is what is meant by assessment informing instruction, not using a single-point standardized measure that informs people outside the classroom how well students take tests.

Modeled Writing

Writing activity occurred every day, without fail, for one and a half hours. Maier never sent children to write without modeling writing first, a practice that reflects her understanding of scaffolding children's learning in their zone of proximal development. Maier's practice of modeling writing consists of five sections: Topic Selection, Drawing, Writing, I likes and Questions/Revision (Larson and Maier, 2000). She used these sections to illustrate her own processes as a writer, to take off the top of her head as Atwell (1998) calls it, and let the students in on what writers think about as they write. Again, the text is real, with a real audience and a real purpose, and the practices she models help the students understand what a reader needs in order to understand what the author is trying to say.

By saying out loud all the possible stories she could write about during *topic selection*, Maier showed that all writers have to decide what to write about and that it is not always an easy choice. She reinforced this idea when she talked to children about developing their own topics lists. Maier began her writing by *drawing* picture clues to the upcoming narrative. She used this as an instructional strategy that oriented students to the writing and provided a scaffold to words in the text. The students excitedly called out what they thought she was drawing and began to make guesses about the story. As soon as the pictures were finished, she began writing (Figure 5.1).

Figure 5.1 Digital video still: writing at the easel

The *writing* portion of this activity was rich in layered instructional tools. As she wrote, Maier read each word as the students read along. They predicted what words she would write next. Reading along with her mirrored what they do together in Morning Message. This modeling was an invaluable resource for the development of orthographic competence, composition strategies, prediction, sentence and paragraph construction, punctuation, spelling and audience awareness; all curriculum elements demanded in the district's literacy curriculum. Maier re-read her text constantly, modeling a writer's strategies of going over a text under construction to monitor whether it makes sense and is flowing smoothly. '*I likes*' followed writing and served as a transition from her writing to the revision section. It was a deliberate scaffold for students to learn to offer positive feedback before critique of someone else's text.

Things really came together here in the *question/revision* segment of modeled writing. Maier provided a space for students as readers to ask questions about her text that, in turn, promote revision. Students came to understand that text was not final and that authors need to account for reader needs as they compose text. Most traditional classrooms teach writing as first draft writing. By this we mean that students focus on writing a story from a story starter in which the first version is the final version. In Maier's classroom, students choose their own topics for writing and produce multiple drafts before making the text public in the Author's Tea (Larson and Maier, 2000).

Student Writing

After modeled writing, students told Maier what they planned on writing about and then headed to their tables to do their own writing. The students moved quickly to independence during student writing time (for example, they moved quickly from dependence on her for assistance to depending on each other to writing independently). Her emphasis on building meaningful and trusting social relations in the classroom contributed to a context for literacy learning that promoted peer interaction as a scaffold for revision. Students' interaction with each other mirrored the modeled writing Maier did with them earlier in the day.

For example, the publication of students' texts (personal narratives, chapter books, poems, memoirs, songs), the sharing of texts across activities (sharing time, Author's Tea, the 'read to three then me' rule), and composing decisions based on an understanding of the role of audience and purpose, all facilitated students' developing their own goals for writing (for example, communication with readers) as they gained in competence (Griffin and Cole, 1984; Larson and Maier, 2000).

Reading

Maier's reading program is as rich, layered and complex as the writing we have just described. There are at least five parts to her reading curriculum: Read Aloud; Shared Reading; Guided Reading; Independent Reading; and the Home reading program (Bag of Books) we described earlier.

Maier's current district requires the use of a packaged reading program in all its elementary schools. She designed her literacy curriculum using this required program, but 'made it her own'. During *Read Aloud*, Maier read a book either she or the students selected. While typically teachers read the book straight through with very little interruption or perhaps introduced by a book walk, Maier commonly stopped to ask questions, let students comment on the book (and make connections to their lives) and/or answer student questions. In *Shared Reading*, Maier used the selected text to teach specific instructional goals. In other words, she used a group reading for instructional purposes. Talk and interaction around the text were specifically planned, although not scripted, to meet the goal/s through her use of the responsive/collaborative script (Gutierrez, 1993) we described earlier. Maier typically constructed the goal/s, but students could come up with goals that she then adopted (Rogoff et al., 2001).

Guided Reading has become a more prominent reading activity in classrooms in the USA, although there is no standard way it is implemented across districts. Again, Maier adapted the packaged version of this activity to what she considers to be best practice. She used the basic framework (Fountas and Pinnell, 1996): a small group of students, strategically grouped based on ability, who read one book and focus on reading strategies. Building on Rogoff's (1990; 2003) concept of guided participation, Maier used flexible grouping that does not necessarily depend on ability grouping. For some guided reading sessions, she grouped along the lines of traditional concepts of ability (for example, beginning, average and exceptional readers). At other times she mixed up abilities and focused the groups on what she called 'word study'. For example, she may have noticed in her ongoing assessment that an exceptional reader was struggling with the same issue (for example, using punctuation marks) as a beginning reader. In this case, she assembled the group with a range of abilities but focused instruction on using punctuation marks. All the students with varying support from her or each other read the same books. Her instructional goal for guided reading groups was to teach reading strategies. She typically selected several books chosen based on student interest, her assessment of reading abilities and skill needed. All the students in each group read all the books. Maier listened while they read, often taking notes or running records to document what students were doing and what they still needed help on.

ANALYSIS OF A SERIES OF LESSONS ON A THEME

One day during the beginning of writing time in her new classroom, the students suggested Maier write a Magic Tree House story about them. This idea evolved into a larger unit that focused on 'reading around the world'. Maier wanted to introduce students to international children's authors as a way to scaffold their transition from personal narrative to more sophisticated writing genres and wove this idea into the children's desire to 'visit' other countries. The goal was for children to read a variety of literature, including non-fiction, on different continents. Given it was winter at the time and very cold outside, students decided they should start with somewhere cold, since they already had the appropriate clothes. Eventually they ended up with the idea of starting with Antarctica. Together they constructed an elaborate series of lessons that included making passports needed for international travel that led to taking a ride to Antarctica on a magic plane (Figure 5.2). She used a large cloth airplane for the imaginary ride to the South Pole.

Figure 5.2 Digital Video Still, Magic Plane Ride

Consistent with sociocultural-historical theory, the students and teacher shared in the construction of activity purposes (Rogoff et al., 2001). Students identified things they might see in Antarctica, suggesting they would find penguins and Eskimos (*sic*), then Maier asked them what they knew about these topics. Once they had established what the students thought they knew (for example, penguins have fur), Maier sent them off to do research in her vast collection of penguin books that includes both fiction and non-fiction. She left it up to students to learn what books would be good resources for learning, knowing that a cute fiction story about a penguin would be less helpful. In this way, Maier scaffolded students taking responsibility for their own learning. Students came back from their research with facts and ideas, learning, for example, that penguins have feathers not fur and that there are no people (other than scientists in special enclaves).

The children took full advantage of her extensive library and became proficient readers. Maier used her intimate knowledge of students and their lives to select books and to design reading events that drew on who the students were. She helped the children make explicit connections to who they were by selecting books that she knew would draw on everyday experiences. This was more than using students 'prior knowledge' in a scripted way – it continually built on the social relations being constructed in this room in a dynamic community of learners.

She carefully integrated the teaching of traditional writing conventions in mini-lessons as she made her own authorship processes explicit for her students in an interactive context in which student knowledge and capabilities as writers and authors were taken seriously (Nystrand, 1997; Rose, 1995). Thus, she did not simply model writing as a discrete technique or set of skills, but modeled authorship as a meaningful writing process constructed in interaction.

Maier has continually attended professional development seminars and workshops both locally and nationally, even 28 years after becoming a teacher. She is often surprised by the lack of interest in continued learning experience her young colleagues express. These various experiences have been incorporated into her curriculum and transformed by her values, beliefs, and teaching experience to form her theory of teaching literacy (Gallas, 1994). She uses these experiences to develop a classroom writing community in which authorship is a key means of participation (Dyson, 1997). In this classroom, authorship is a mutually constituted, goal-directed activity that changes and is changed by students' and teacher's engagement with texts. Future research might focus on how the tools for thinking change and are changed by their use (Rogoff, 2003).

Participation in literacy activity in this classroom is active and includes both central and peripheral participation in and with multiple forms of texts (students' and teacher's oral and written texts, novels, children's literature, textbooks, leveled books, music, video, and computer texts). The 'everyday-ness' and predictability of the activities Maier and her students construct supports the co-construction of literacy practices. Maier uses her knowledge of the role of talk and interaction in literacy learning in constructing her literacy curriculum. Students are free to talk, ask questions and write (and share) who they are with others. Making meaning in her classroom was not an individual process of text ownership (Dyson, 1997) but a dialogic process rooted in interaction with and around text (Erickson, 1996; Nystrand, 1997).

Barbara Rogoff is an internationally known scholar whose research forms the foundations of sociocultural-historical theory. In the closing section of this chapter, Rogoff responds to several questions we posed about Maier's practice and sociocultural-historical theory.

INTERVIEW WITH BARBARA ROGOFF

WHAT ASPECTS OF THIS CASE STUDY DO YOU FEEL REFLECT THE MAIN TENETS OF SOCIOCULTURAL-HISTORICAL THEORY?

I was particularly struck by the extent to which Maier embedded writing lessons within the goal of communication, thereby making the use of writing tools a means rather than an end in itself. The students learned the format for letter openings and closings as a way to exchange information with their teacher, not as isolated facts with unknown purpose. Also, Maier routinely modeled the processes that she wanted the students to learn, bringing them inside the use of longstanding and often mysterious practices (such as topic selection, drafting and editing). By thinking aloud in situations related to the ones the students would face, she allowed them to view her process – one important way for people to find their way into a new practice.

Maier's development of classroom traditions that serve the students across multiple contexts (such as the letter format that she used for whole-class morning messages as well as in her notes to individuals) provides students with structures that bring them closer to the mature forms of the practices that they are beginning to participate in. Her word hunts, using real communicative text, coach the students in difficult aspects of decoding, addressing skills that are often isolated from their use, through a collaborative assistance role rather than the common drillmaster role. Her assessment focuses on ascertaining what the students need next and how she can assist them in the next steps, in line with dynamic forms of assessment based on the concept of the zone of proximal development.

Maier's approach is an inspirational example of a particular form of guided participation (one that is quite compatible with the examples given in Rogoff et al., 2001). Because the concept of guided participation is often misunderstood, I would like to clarify that this concept does not specify a particular form of engagement but is instead intended to help us focus on examining a variety of forms of engagement, of which this is one. Others include the sorts of engagement that occur as children observe everyday activities to which they have access but which are not intended to instruct them, the kind of learning that occurs as children participate in sanctioned and unsanctioned ways in recitation-and-test classrooms, and even the kind of learning that occurs when youngsters learn to participate in illegal activities through their participation in and observation of these. For discussion of the variety of forms of guided participation, see Chapter 8 of *The Cultural Nature of Human Development* (Rogoff, 2003).

Most of the description of Maier's practices focuses on how she interacts with the children and the formats she designs to help them become skilled users of cultural tools of writing. There is a little information provided that touches on other key aspects of sociocultural-historical theory – the historical, cultural, institutional nature of Maier's practices. She apparently developed some of her practices by appropriating aspects of professional development seminars in which she participated over 28 years.

A more complete sociocultural-historical analysis of this case would also examine the broader historical basis of Maier's practice and the children's involvement. Such analysis could focus on such features as the children's compulsory attendance at school for much of their childhood; the uses of literacy in the children's home community and the children's inclusion or exclusion in community literacy practices; the bureaucratic structure, requirements and educational policies of Maier's school, school district and nation; the formats for writing available in Maier's century (clay tablets? yellow lined paper? computers?); the way that Maier's own opportunities to learn were structured in her own schooling from K-12 through her university classes in literature, geography and pedagogy; the political structure that has encouraged or barred the participation of Maier's and her students' parents in the practices she is teaching; and so on. As I discuss in Rogoff (2003), often sociocultural-historical theory is taken up for what it offers in examining ongoing social interaction, but the theory also emphasizes the cultural, institutional and historical aspects that contribute to all moments of learning and social interaction.

WHAT DO YOU SEE AS THE MOST IMPORTANT CONTRIBUTION SOCIOCULTURAL-HISTORICAL THEORY CAN MAKE TO CLASSROOM PRACTICE?

To open our eyes to the implicit, tacit ways in which we and our students participate in practices that experienced practitioners may take for granted. If we are more aware of the practices and how they are structured and how people begin to participate in them, as teachers we can more effectively design our classroom arrangements and other aspects of instruction in support of easing students into the traditions of thought and creative thinking that schools are supposed to promote.

WHAT IDEAS DO YOU HAVE TO HELP TEACHERS UNDERSTAND THE FOUNDATIONS OF SOCIOCULTURAL-HISTORICAL THEORY?

Together with teachers, parents, students and administrators involved in an innovative public school that has contributed immensely to my ideas, I have written a collaborative book examining how people learn as a community (*Learning Together: Children and Adults in a School Community* [Rogoff et al., 2001]). We hope to spark readers' ideas about learning by considering key principles of learning as a community. We use examples from our practice to discuss what it means to form community in classrooms and schools, how children learn together with adults, how teachers and parents learn together with children and with each other, and how the community as a whole learns over time from their efforts to create an approach to learning that is compatible with the ideas of this chapter.

HOW DO YOU HELP TEACHERS IMPLEMENT A SOCIOCULTURAL-HISTORICAL THEORY FRAMEWORK IN THEIR CLASSROOMS?

Well, in addition to contributing to the book *Learning Together*, which has this as one of its major goals, I try to model the principles of learning as a community in the university classes that I teach. If a key principle in people's learning is that people learn from their participation, then it is a major goal of university education to structure our classes so that students have the opportunity to participate in the ways that we hope that they themselves will carry out in their subsequent opportunities to aid others' learning.

In classes as large as 140 students, I try to serve as a guide to the students (rather than as a boss or police officer) and I foster discussion in the class as a whole so they can make use of resources provided by their classmates.

I provide many writing assignments that try to build on students' interests in ways that require them to engage with the main concepts I want them to learn as well as providing me with information regarding their understanding and needs for clarification, and I model the kind of communication and scholarly inquiry approaches I want them to develop.

This is a major challenge at the university level, as most of the students are very used to other approaches so they need support in learning to learn in this manner. (It seems to help them catch on when I tell them that I'm trying to teach a large class as I would a small class.) With appropriate support in getting the hang of this changed structure, students often flourish in ways that extend well beyond the immediate subject matter of the course.

CONCLUSION

Sociocultural-historical theory affords a comprehensive way to find new practices (such as some of the new practices associated with new technologies). This framework offers tools for research and analysis of literacy that foreground culture and history in unique ways and will highlight historical practices and structures that impact literacy learning in specific contexts. Furthermore, sociocultural-historical theory offers literacy researchers an authentic way to connect micro and macro analyses. There has been a tendency to focus on individual cases and make claims about communities from microanalytic studies. Using this framework helps to focus on multiple communities and practice to add complexity to our understanding of human activity, including literacy activity.

In this chapter, we have briefly described the historical foundations of sociocultural-historical theory and grounded that explanation in a case study of veteran first grade teacher Maryrita Maier. The interview with Barbara Rogoff highlighted the ways in which Maier's practice interfaced with the theoretical framework and pointed out some limitations of current uses of sociocultural-historical theory. Having finished our outlining of four theoretical frameworks for understanding literacy learning, we turn now to the task of bringing these frameworks together in the next chapter, Chapter 6, and to understanding the implications for teacher education and research in the final chapter, Chapter 7.

NOTES

1 See Rogoff et al. (2001) for an in-depth discussion of sociocultural-historical theory and teaching written with and by teachers and students.

2 See Cole, 1996; Lee and Smagorinsky, 2000; Rogoff, 1990; 2003; Wertsch, 1991; Wertsch et al., 1995, for in-depth discussion of the origins and theoretical foundations of socio-cultural-historical theory.

3 See Gee et al. (1996) for discussion of the often conflicting nature of multiple discourses.

4 See Rogoff et al. (2001) for examples of the application of a community of learners concept in an alternative public school.

CHAPTER 6

Understanding How the Frameworks Work Together

This chapter details the relationships and connections that may be made across the frameworks described thus far in the book. We will pay particular attention to how the frameworks may work together to enable educators to achieve several goals:

1 Make active and meaningful use of children's language and literacy practices as resources for curriculum.

2 Understand literacy as a critical social practice and its potential for change.

3 Provide a pedagogical approach which fosters communities of learners.

4 Plan classroom activities that embed meaningful opportunities to engage in the analysis and construction of multimodal texts.

5 Utilize teaching approaches that move beyond the 'false tension between abstracting the codes of language and learning their application for meaningful purposes' (Hall, 2003: 324).

These goals offer a means of designing, planning, implementing and studying meaningful literacy curricula, in spite of the increasingly reductionist pressure to teach literacy as a set of decontextualized skills. They provide a framework for the analysis of the case study classrooms, in that we interrogate the practice outlined in previous chapters and identify how the teachers strive, in their various ways, to meet these goals, informed by the four theoretical models outlined in each chapter. Initially, however, we consider the relationship between these models.

MULTIDISCIPLINARY PERSPECTIVES

The theories we have discussed thus far in the book work together to form a comprehensive theory of learning, language and literacy. New Literacy Studies facilitates an ethnographic understanding of literacies in use across contexts. Understanding how teachers and students construct and use literacy in and out of school will help to disrupt the deficit model hegemony that remains dominant in contemporary schooling and contributes to inequality (Gutierrez and Rogoff, 2003; Irvine and Larson, 2001; Larson, 2003; Woods, 2004). New technologies are changing how we use and interpret literacies, and for what purposes. Studying new literacies has opened up exciting research possibilities and new pedagogical spaces that build on children's language and literacy practices across contexts (Lankshear and Knobel, 2003a; Marsh, 2005). Critical literacy provides a framework for action, or praxis, that uses literacies to activate social and political transformations (Comber and Simpson, 2001). Finally, sociocultural-historical theories of learning offer teachers a meaningful understanding of how learning happens in and out of school and complements both NLS, critical literacy and techno-literacy by affording teachers and researchers authentic strategies for actively using students' social, cultural and linguistic resources without reducing them to a simplified series of classroom lessons (Gutierrez and Rogoff, 2003; Irvine and Larson, 2001). By viewing learning as changing participation in a culturally valued activity that is mediated by interaction and cultural tools for thinking, such as literacy, teachers can construct authentic contexts for learning that prepare students for participation in a global information and communication economy.

Viewed in this way, it is clear that each of the theoretical frameworks offers a distinct way of conceptualizing literacy within educational contexts. However, that does not mean that each stands alone, unaffected by the others. Teachers may draw simultaneously from each of the frameworks in different ways. Figure 6.1 illustrates the potential relationship of the frameworks we have discussed.

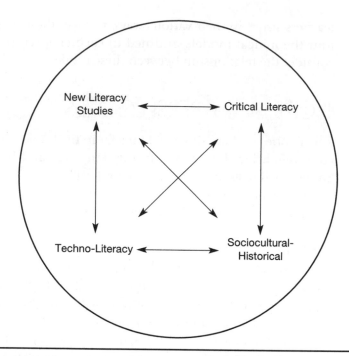

Figure 6.1 Multidisciplinary theoretical framework

Using Figure 6.1, we can begin to think about how the theoretical frame-works afford us a way to 'see' classrooms, either as teachers developing and implementing curriculum or as researchers developing, conducting and analyzing data in research. We view this diagram as representative of a continuum of locations in which teachers and researchers can position themselves differently at different times for different purposes, yet remain theoretically consistent. For example, Maier begins her thinking about curriculum and pedagogy from a sociocultural-historical perspective that includes a definition of literacy used in New Literacy Studies, but has begun to move toward understanding how to use digital literacies. Maier's curriculum and pedagogical decisions are grounded in this multidisciplinary theoretical framework. Her use of workshop approaches to teaching writing, for example, arises out of her understanding of authentic audiences and purposes for writing. She uses a workshop approach to teach school-based literacy in ways that do not sacrifice children's own repertoires of literacy practices (Gutierrez and Rogoff, 2003). Gatto uses workshop approaches to teach both school-based literacy and out-of-school literacies, or authentic professional literacies (videoconferencing, email, scientific observation). Beginning from an NLS perspective, she draws on all the other frameworks to construct and enact her science-based curriculum. Malden's work draws on an understanding of the nature of literacy in a digital world, but is also informed by sociocultural-historical learning theory in that, in her classroom, the child is identified as an active participant in a community of learners in which knowledge is co-constructed. Vasquez's practice is grounded in a strong commitment to the key principles of critical literacy, but she also draws on other aspects of Figure 6.1 to inform her pedagogy. In particular, the emphasis in NLS on the importance of offering a curriculum that reflects authentic sociocultural literacy practices can be seen to permeate Vasquez's practice.

SIMILARITIES AND DIFFERENCES

Figure 6.1 suggests that theoretical models of literacy do not operate in a vacuum and, indeed, there are many overlapping features of the models discussed in this book. All four models emphasize the sociocultural contexts in which literacy operates; all four position the learner as an active agent in the construction of meaning. However, each theoretical model emphasizes a slightly different facet of the complex dynamic between learner, text and the possible involvement of a teacher in any classroom literacy event. Figure 6.2 represents this dynamic, which also illustrates how these classroom literacy events are informed by wider sociocultural literacy practices. The differences between the four theoretical models in relation to Figure 6.2 may offer theoretical and pedagogical spaces for change that researchers can investigate to move particular aspects of literacy studies forward.

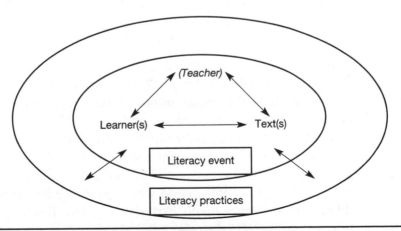

Figure 6.2 Literacy events and practices in classrooms

If we consider Figure 6.2 in relation to each of the theoretical models of literacy discussed in this book, the differences between them might become more transparent. It could be argued, for example, that New Literacy

Studies have traditionally placed a greater emphasis on literacy practices than other aspects of this diagram (Street, 2005). In contrast, critical literacy theory has emphasized the importance of what happens between learner and text in a critical literacy event, of course recognizing that that interaction is dependent upon wider sociopolitical literacy practices. Sociocultural-historical learning theory has focused primarily on the interactions between learners, and learners and teachers. Lankshear and Knobel, in Chapter 3, suggested that new technological practices outside school are rarely reflected in the kinds of literacy events taking place within classrooms and so the arrows that relate a two-way process between these concentric circles are, in fact, problematic. The fact that there is much overlap between the models should not cloud these differences between them, nor should it mean that educators do not need to understand the distinctions as they meld together a practice rooted in the dynamic offered by the interaction of the models. Ultimately, what is important is for teachers to recognize the affordances of the various theoretical models and to draw as necessary from each in order to inform research, theory and practice.

In order to examine the features of each theoretical model in more depth, we have indicated the key tenets of each in relation to the different categories identified in Figure 6.2 – learner, teacher, texts, literacy events and literacy practices. We do so to distinguish the individual features of each, but also to emphasize the relationship between these categories and to ground the theoretical models in the context of use by learners and teachers in authentic events and practices. Using Table 6.1, educators can begin to locate their own positions within the frameworks and make connections across frameworks as they identify similarities.

Table 6.1 illustrates that the models have both commonalities and differences, as suggested previously. All the models identify a range of literacies used for a variety of purposes and to a variety of audiences. Learners are seen as active in constructing purposes and consequences of literacy. Leadership and expertise are shared among learners and teachers. All theories point to a complex notion of text as a multimodal, ideological tool. Literacy events and practices are nested concepts that afford a multifaceted understanding of micro and macro processes and structures. Key differences, although these differences are not mutually exclusive, nor can they be reduced to simple binaries, include: (1) the overt political praxis component of critical literacy is not shared by all; (2) the emphasis on learning and development of sociocultural-historical theory is not explicit in all models; and (3) the disjuncture between literacy practices in out-of-school contexts and what takes place in classrooms is highlighted more strongly in relation to techno-literacy than in

Table 6.1 Some Key Features of Each Theoretical Model

	Learners	Teacher	Texts	Literacy events	Literacy practices
New Literacy Studies	Learners use literacy in a variety of forms (multiple literacies) for a variety of purposes across contexts, both formal and informal.	Teachers are facilitators of learners' use of literacy for a variety of purposes and participation in literacy events and practices.	The concept of multiliteracies implies that texts are multimodal and multipurposed.	Literacy events are conceived as occasions where texts (in a variety of forms) are central to participation.	Literacy practices may include literacy events, but also include larger social, cultural, historical and political practices.
Techno-literacy	Many learners are already competent in a range of techno-literacy practices, but this is often not recognized or valued in schools. Learners need opportunities to extend their competences and understanding.	Emphasis on teacher as guide in navigating resources, co-constructor of knowledge (this vision is hampered by the fact that some teachers lack confidence and skills in relation to new technologies).	Texts are multimodal, drawing on the affordances of various digital and non-digital media.	Literacy events require learners to have an understanding of the affordances of different modes and place an emphasis on design as well as analysis of audiences and purposes.	Literacy practices are informed by the rapid developments in technology occurring within contemporary societies. These are creating fundamental epistemological and ontological shifts that are not reflected in schooled practices.
Critical literacy	Learners are positioned as active agents in relation to texts and social practices.	Teachers facilitate the development of learners' understandings of the way in which they are positioned in relation to texts and social practices.	Texts are ideological constructions, informed by authorial intent and issues relating to power.	Literacy events involve deconstruction of the ideological content of texts and production of texts that inform critical understanding.	Literacy practices are shaped by, and shape, social, cultural, political and economic contexts in which power is the central dynamic.

Table 6.1 continued

	Learners	Teacher	Texts	Literacy events	Literacy practices
Sociocultural-historical theory	Learners are active agents in taking responsibility for their learning and constructing goals and purposes for literacy learning.	Teachers are facilitators of learners' changing participation in goal-oriented activity. They take leadership in designing activities, but share construction of purposes with learners. Teachers are also considered learners.	Texts are tools used to mediate learning for a variety of purposes.	Literacy events are activities in which text as a tool plays a key role in mediating learning.	Literacy practices may be understood as broader sociocultural repertoires of practices used to mediate learning in goal-oriented activity.

the other theoretical models. Thus, in distinguishing both the significant differences between the models and identifying the overlaps, we are not suggesting that teachers should position themselves as grounding their practice in one of these theoretical models exclusively, nor do we think that the reality of classroom life is such that it would be an impossible task to identify different conceptualizations of literacy. Rather, we suggest that the task of developing one's praxis is a constant interplay between various theoretical models and classroom practice, and those educators who are able to reflect in a critical way on their underpinning theoretical frameworks are the ones most likely to offer the kind of transformative pedagogies displayed by the teachers who are featured in this book.

THEORETICAL CONSISTENCY IN RESEARCH

Table 6.1 can also inform the way in which each of the theoretical models can frame research, research that takes place in classrooms, in out-of-school contexts and the in-between spaces. In Chapter 1, we considered the relationship between theory and research (see Figure 1.2). Each of the four models discussed in this book can be used either separately or in combination to develop a theoretical framework for research or inform analysis. Examples of research studies which foreground one model in particular are as follows:

1 New Literacy Studies: Larson (2005) and Larson and Gatto (2004; 2005) use an NLS framework to analyze ethnographic data gathered in a three-year study of Gatto and her students' language and literacy practices. Their analyses show how learning travels across interactional contexts and that learning is not located in an in/out binary. The recently completed dissertation research of Davidson (2005) and Woods (2004) both foreground analyses of literacy as a social practice in early childhood literacy events and connect this perspective to current reductionist mandates in Australia.

2 Techno-literacy: in Davies (forthcoming), the literacy practices of teenagers as they engage in chatroom discourse are analyzed using a framework that emphasizes the epistemological and ontological changes taking place due to advances in technology. Davies outlines the way in which users of a website devoted to the software package Babyz (Mindscape, 1995) develop shared discourses in which rules and procedures to be used in the group and varied aspects of subject matter are collectively understood. She draws on Gee's concept of 'affinity spaces' (Gee, 2004) to delineate how the participants create these discourses and how shared social practices bind the group together in sociological, as well as semiotic and linguistic, ways. Davies explores how far these sophisticated practices are situated from classrooms and argues that 'These multimodal developments are ones which evolve from new social practices created by the existence of a new social space which occupies an intangible but highly significant position in the digitally developed world; they therefore need a place on the curriculum quite urgently' (Davies, forthcoming). Although Davies does develop a theoretical framework for this analysis that is informed by multidisciplinary research and scholarship, her key tools for understanding the data are drawn from the field of literacy and new technologies (Gee, 2003; 2004; Kress, 2003; Lankshear and Knobel, 2003a).

3 Critical literacy: in Janks and Comber (forthcoming), the researchers outline how children in two schools, one in Adelaide and one in South Africa, produced alphabet books to exchange, books that featured aspects of their lives and neighborhood. Janks and Comber draw from a critical literacy perspective to

illustrate how these alphabet books developed children's political understandings of their own situation, as well as informed them about the daily lives of children in another part of the world. The children in South Africa, for example, included commentaries on the prevalence of AIDS in their community, and outlined the inadequacies of the public health system. The children in the Adelaide school reflected, amongst other things, on issues relating to safety in their neighborhood. Janks and Comber suggest that critical literacy involving knowledge exchange between global partners such as this is 'important because the learning that is accomplished by seeing someone else's poverty, school, pedagogies, has the power to disrupt the taken-for-granted knowledges that might otherwise fence us in' (Janks and Comber, forthcoming). Another reading of the data in this project might have emphasized the multimodal nature of the children's text production, as the children produced models, made maps and took digital photographs. Although the authors discuss this, it is not a major unit of analysis; rather, the emphasis is placed on understanding how the activity contributed to the use of literacy for political ends.

4 Sociocultural-historical theory: Anne Dyson's research (1997; 2002) in early childhood is the most well-known example of understanding literacy from a sociocultural perspective. Research examining literacy in childhood that uses the more recent framework articulated by Rogoff (2003) is more difficult to find. Gutierrez and Stone (2002) used a sociocultural-historical framework to understand the consequences of what they termed 'hypermediating' on literacy learning. Enciso (2005) examines the meanings and representations of history in sociocultural theory by working with teachers to analyze the gaps and absences in a mythological continuous narrative. She argues that a more critical sociocultural theory will displace the traditional historical narrative of universal (common) knowledge that teachers can use to foster the development of counter-narratives.

Of course, there are many excellent examples of research studies that draw extensively from each of the four theoretical frameworks; we have chosen the above simply to illustrate the kinds of research that reflect each model in a clear and distinct manner. Nevertheless, all is not straightforward, of course; each of these studies also engages with aspects of other theoretical models in various ways. Key tenets of New Literacy Studies, for example, can be seen in all these studies. As with our discussion about the four theoretical frameworks in relation to teaching, researchers need also to draw on each framework at different times, for different purposes and in various ways, and to recognize the ways in which they overlap and integrate. The important factor is that as researchers, we are also clear about the distinct affordances of each of the models.

EDUCATIONAL GOALS

We would suggest that one of the aims of developing a sound theoretical underpinning to research, policy and practice is to achieve well-formulated goals that advance knowledge and understanding and effect social change. In the next section, we move on to consider the five goals outlined in the introduction to this chapter. These goals are central to contemporary educational practice and each of the case studies offers examples of how teachers can strive towards their achievement, despite constraints posed by official curriculum mandates and limited resources. Here, we draw out the key features of the teachers' practices that illustrate each of the goals.

1 ACTIVE AND MEANINGFUL USE OF CHILDREN'S LANGUAGE AND LITERACY PRACTICES AS RESOURCES FOR CURRICULUM

All the theoretical models emphasize the need to embed authentic literacy practices within the curriculum. In the case of New Literacy Studies, researchers have advocated the use of extended ethnographic accounts of learners' lives outside educational institutions to inform curricula (Hull and Schultz, 2002). Proponents of new technologies have stressed how important it is to build on the extensive experiences many children now have with digital literacy practices outside the classroom (Lankshear and Knobel, 2003a). A major feature of critical literacy theory is the extent to which it recognizes the value of building on children's own linguistic and literary repertoires in the classroom in order that schools do not privilege canonical texts (Comber, 2003). Finally, by focusing on 'people's history of engagement in practices of cultural communities' (Gutierrez and Rogoff, 2003: 21), sociocultural-historical theory shifts educators' attention away from a focus on individual traits to look instead at how people live culturally (Moll, 2000). This more complex understanding of repertoires of practice affords educators a means for *seeing* cultural practices and for *using* these practices in the construction and implementation of curricula.

All four of the case studies teachers illustrate how this particular goal can be met. For example, Gatto takes literacy learning beyond the classroom. She combines authentic learning experiences with professional practices in a way that gives her students' opportunities to change their participation in multiple forms of literacy across a variety of contexts. Her science-based curriculum fosters excitement and engagement in her students. This excitement could be seen as students tracked the growth and changes in trees in Ellison Park over the course of a year. Each student kept a scientific journal that documented a tree's changes over fall, winter and spring. They communicated their findings with a partner classroom in Kentucky using videoconferencing and email, both practices commonly used in business in the twenty-first century. Gatto constructs authentic pedagogical spaces for students to use their home and community literacies in inquiry projects that have a social action component.

Similarly, Malden is aware of the digital literacy practices the children in her class engage in outside the classroom. They regularly use email, instant messaging and chatrooms, and this knowledge informed their interactions with children from another school as they collaborated on the planning of presentations. In addition, the children reflected on their literacy and language practices in the home as they took digital photographs of the icons, texts and artifacts most meaningful to them, such as the Koran, favorite books and popular CD-ROMs (see Figures 4.2 and 4.3 in Chapter 4). This use of children's own cultural interests should not, however, be reduced to the mere appropriation of children's interests for the achievement of narrow ends, for example using Pokémon characters, popular anime figures related to a computer game and television program, to create phonics worksheets. Rather, students' own practices should be embedded in meaningful ways – ways that enable them to interrogate those practices using the analytical tools they use for other texts, ways which respect the pleasures they derive from such activities.

This authentic respect for children's own cultural practices can be seen in Vasquez's work. Vasquez, in her provision of a daily class meeting, allowed children to bring to the classroom issues and concerns that were of current interest to them. Rather than push these interests to the margins of daily life, Vasquez enabled them to become center-stage and promote a range of curriculum activities. Children's experiences of the school barbecue did not begin and end with the barbecue itself, but became the focus for political action which promoted change.

Maier uses children's culture as content for writing. She models how an author selects topics using her own life events, then facilitates children's use of family events or popular culture in student writing time. She learns from the children about what is 'current', thereby positioning students as experts and herself as a learner. Focusing on learning as the center of literacy pedagogy is consistent with sociocultural-historical theory's emphasis on both adults and children as learners (Rogoff et al., 2001).

2 UNDERSTANDING LITERACY AS A CRITICAL SOCIAL PRACTICE AND ITS POTENTIAL FOR CHANGE

As with the first goal, it should be noted that all four of the theoretical frameworks analyzed in this book emphasize the potential for literacy to act as a critical social practice that can effect change. Street, for example, suggests that detailed ethnographic studies can be used to inform policy, citing work in Nepal as an example:

> The Community Literacy Project Nepal aims to do precisely this. Based on a spirit of engagement between theory and practice, academic and applied concerns, it aims to make a contribution at the interface, clarifying conceptual issues, and enhancing knowledge on the one hand and aiding policy making and program building on the other (cf. Rogers, 1992). (2003: 8)

Researchers focused on techno-literacy practices suggest that this work can effect social change on a large scale (Rheingold, 2003) as communities find new and exciting ways to communicate and share thoughts and strategies. For example, some have suggested that the increasingly popular activity of 'blogging' (creating a web log, a form of online diary) has the potential to provide a source of uncensored information on a range of matters and can impact on the political climate (Lankshear and Knobel, 2003b). Sociocultural-historical theory is not typically associated with the kind of political praxis of critical literacy; however, by bringing a complex notion of culture to the forefront of analyzing literacy practices, it affords the transformation of the deficit model ideology so prominent in schools (Gutierrez and Rogoff, 2003).

The tenets of critical literacy as critical social action can be seen in Gatto's classroom. For example, her students wrote letters to the Mexican government with suggestions for preserving the monarch butterfly habitat after they learned that commercialization might endanger the habitat ecology (Gatto, 2001). Students internalized the use of literacy as a tool for social and political action. The summer after the completion of the three-year loop, Gatto received a letter from a student asking her if there were any grants he could apply for so he could try and improve the school lunches at his new school. Maier's own resistance to packaged pedagogy and her continuous challenging of reductionist definitions of literacy may be considered representative of a critical literacy stance. Malden was concerned that pupils in her class used literacy to pursue critical goals. In the case identified, that involved ensuring that student teachers had an insider perspective on young children's cultural practices.

However, although all the theoretical models emphasize the way in which literacy should effect change in various ways, it is critical literacy that has made most impact in terms of offering practical models for such work. In Vasquez's classroom, children used literacy to challenge established practices and effect change. The children, through carefully prepared letter-writing, were able to guarantee the provision of vegetarian food at the school barbecue in future years, and the school library had to reconsider its book collection in the light of the children's campaigning. These children had a powerful understanding of the potential literacy has to transform the political and social landscape.

3 A PEDAGOGICAL APPROACH WHICH FOSTERS COMMUNITIES OF LEARNERS

The development of a community of learners is important if teachers and students are to construct classroom spaces in which peer tutoring and collaboration establish meaningful contexts for learning. Nevertheless, this is not to suggest that the notion of 'community' should indicate unification and lack of dissension, given the differences in power and status that learners bring to the site of learning (Lewis, 2001). Rather, the development of authentic learning communities relies on the degree of trust that can be built up between participants, trust that will enable challenges to normalized power relations and social practices within classrooms. In relation to the four theoretical models outlined in this book, all embed recognition of the importance of building such communities, but it is, perhaps, in socio-cultural-historical theory that the main emphasis on the social construction of knowledge can be found.

For example, Maier bases her writing on her own writing practices, with an emphasis on personal narrative at the beginning, then bridges to other genres. This choice is based on her understanding of children's writing development and the requirements of the local school district and the state department of education. She does not teach to the test, but her careful analysis of what is tested helps her plan what she calls a humane way to teach literacy. As Chapter 5 has detailed, Maier used a complexly layered literacy curriculum rooted in workshop approaches to teaching literacy. Her students learn to write personal narratives, poems, chapter books that include all traditional sections of a book (table of contents, about the author, dedication, and so on), letters and announcements. These text genres all have authentic audiences and purposes that contribute to Maier's overarching goal of constructing a trusting community of learners.

4 CLASSROOM ACTIVITIES THAT EMBED MEANINGFUL OPPORTUNITIES TO ENGAGE IN THE ANALYSIS AND CONSTRUCTION OF MULTIMODAL TEXTS

As suggested in Chapter 1 of this book, traditional literacy practices have focused too heavily on the analysis and construction of written texts. Students have had too few opportunities to construct and analyze texts that utilize a range of modes, activities that would offer a reflection of the rich textual life outside school walls. However, despite the emphasis within New Literacy Studies on the development of meaningful literacy activities within educational settings, there has, until recently, been a lack of attention to multimodalities (Lankshear and Knobel, 2003a). This can also be said of two of the other theoretical frameworks discussed in this book, critical literacy and sociocultural-historical theory, although there are now accounts emerging of classroom practice in which critical literacy activities have drawn on different modes (Nixon and Comber, 2005; Vasquez, 2004b). However, by the very nature of the range of modes involved in techno-literacy practices, this strand of theory and practice has consistently recognized that different modes offer various affordances that can be taken up in diverse ways by text analyzers and producers (Cope and Kalantzis, 2000; Kress, 2003; Lankshear and Knobel, 2003a). In the case studies outlined in this book, Malden provided children in her class with an opportunity to create a range of texts that drew on their knowledge of digital literacy practices. Multimodal presentations incorporated text, still and moving images, and sound files. The production of such texts involved the critique of a range of sources, with students needing to make a range of judgments about all kinds of texts. These processes were embedded within a meaningful activity in which students created presentations based on their own lives and made for a specific audience.

Gatto uses multimodal literacies extensively in her classroom as she and her students communicate across time and space with partner classrooms in various parts of the USA. Her science-based curriculum embeds modal variation across content areas and uses multiple literacies for research and communication of ideas. Maier's students use traditional and electronic modes for research on a variety of topics across the curriculum. The case study of Vasquez's classroom outlined the importance of incorporating multimodal texts from real-life contexts into the curriculum. Although the examples given focused on letter writing, Vasquez did emphasize that the 'Learning Wall' contained a wide range of texts that included photographs, maps and Internet printouts.

All four cases studies also indicated the relationship between production and analysis of multimodal texts. Classrooms that focus on one at the expense of the other do not offer pupils sufficiently balanced curriculum opportunities and do not allow children to develop the ability to apply the skills and knowledge developed in a productive activity to an analytical one (and vice versa).

5 TEACHING APPROACHES THAT MOVE BEYOND THE 'FALSE TENSION BETWEEN ABSTRACTING THE CODES OF LANGUAGE AND LEARNING THEIR APPLICATION FOR MEANINGFUL PURPOSES' (HALL, 2003: 324)

All the theoretical traditions outlined in this book have offered challenges to the psycholinguistic, skills-based notions of literacy which permeated educational practice throughout the twentieth century. However, this is not to set up a simplistic dichotomy between a skills-based model and these frameworks. No one is suggesting that classroom practice has to be either/ or – either focused on learning the codes of language or applying these codes in meaningful ways that reflect literacy as a social practice. All the case studies have illuminated how teachers can achieve both of these aims and, indeed, integrate them seamlessly into curricula in which children acquire a variety of relevant skills, knowledge and understanding in a range of authentic practices for a ranges of purposes.

CONCLUSION

The five goals outlined here are, of course, not exhaustive. They are not intended to provide a limiting framework for practice but, instead, they should offer a means to begin rethinking literacy curricula that have, too often and in too many countries, restricted teachers' practices. The case studies in this book provide a few snapshots of 'real-life' practice, but can only offer glimpses into new, authentic kinds of pedagogy and curricula. It will be important, in the years ahead, to build on the now extensive body of knowledge in relation to each of the theoretical models outlined in this book and to translate these models into complex and vibrant classroom practice, which will itself transform the theories. In the final chapter, we elaborate on the implications of a multidisciplinary theoretical framework for research, teaching and teacher education in the early and primary years.

CHAPTER 7

Implications for Teacher Education and Literacy Research

This closing chapter discusses implications of the theories presented in this book for teacher education and literacy research. We argue that initial teacher education needs to explore theoretical frameworks underpinning contemporary curricula in order for novice teachers to ground practice in a clear understanding of various models and that professional development for in-service (for example, practising or experienced) teachers needs to incorporate models of action research which enable engagement with such theories in the context of classrooms. We close the chapter with a discussion of the implications for future research and policy.

IMPLICATIONS FOR IN-SERVICE TEACHERS

While we agree with Knobel and Lankshear in Chapter 4 that the goal of research and theory is not to simply 'apply' ideas to practice, we do feel that teachers benefit by understanding how theory plays out in their practice and what their theories are. When presented with theoretical concepts or ideas based on research, some teachers respond with reasons why they cannot use theory in their practice, no matter what theoretical position is described. They tend not to conceive of their current practice as theoretically grounded. The hegemony of traditional autonomous literacy and educational psychology is not recognized or questioned. Teachers offer very real and legitimate reasons about external demands, teaching to standards and accountability measures being chief among them. However, a key argument made by all the teachers whose work is featured in this book is that it is possible to integrate good classroom practice with the requirements imposed by external demands. The next section uses the New York State Language Arts Standards as one example of the way in which official curriculum discourse can be appropriated for a more critical approach to literacy education.

The New York State Board of Regents adopted A New Compact for Learning in 1991 that provided the basis for establishing learning standards for the states K-12 students[1] (ages 5–11). This document established standardized criteria for assessing and reporting student achievement that focused on four general concepts of reading, writing, listening and speaking. Establishing the standards, listed in Table 7.1, and the accompanying achievement objectives represented a shift in focus from content to student performance. The Regents claimed that this shift allowed for greater instructional uniformity, which was seen as a positive outcome.

Table 7.1 New York State Language Arts Standards
(http://www.emsc.nysed.gov/ciai/ela/elastandards/elamap.html, accessed 27 July 2004)

STANDARD 1	STANDARD 2
Students will read, write, listen, and speak for information and understanding.	Students will read, write, listen, and speak for literary response and expression.
As listeners and readers, students will collect data, facts, and ideas, discover relationships, concepts, and generalizations; and use knowledge generated from oral, written, and electronically produced texts. As speakers and writers, they will use oral and written language to acquire, interpret, apply, and transmit information.	Students will read and listen to oral, written and electronically produced texts and performances, relate texts and performances to their own lives, and develop an understanding of the diverse social, historical, and cultural dimensions the texts and performances represent. As speakers and writers, students will use oral and written language for self-expression and artistic creation.

STANDARD 3	STANDARD 4
Students will read, write, listen, and speak for critical analysis and evaluation.	Students will read, write, listen, and speak for social interaction.
As listeners and readers, students will analyze experiences, ideas, information, and issues presented by others using a variety of established criteria. As speakers and writers, they will present, in oral and written language and from a variety of perspectives, their opinions and judgments on experiences, ideas, information and issues.	Students will use oral and written language for effective social communication with a wide variety of people. As readers and listeners, they will use the social communications of others to enrich their understanding of people and their views.

The first thing that seems obvious when looking at these standards is that there is nothing explicitly inconsistent with any of the theories we have presented. Furthermore, as we have suggested, if a teacher grounds her/his practice in a sound theoretical base, the resultant curriculum will be meaningful, engaging and relevant, and the external constraints such as the standards will be moot.

As an indicative example of this process, we use two instances from the case studies and relate them to one of the standards (Table 7.2). Chapter 3 outlined how Malden's students used the information they had gathered on children's interests and identities to inform an oral presentation to pre-service teachers. In Chapter 5, we examined how Maier's students used multiple sources of texts and modes of presentation to gather and discuss information about Antarctica for the 'magic plane ride'.

Table 7.2 Relating classroom practice to the New York State Language Arts Standards

Standard	Examples of classroom practice
Students will read, write, listen, and speak for information and understanding As listeners and readers, students will collect data, facts, and ideas, discover relationships, concepts, and generalizations; and use knowledge generated from oral, written, and electronically produced texts. As speakers and writers, they will use oral and written language to acquire, interpret, apply, and transmit information.	■ Malden's pupils used the presentation they had developed on their interests to make a presentation to pre-service teachers about children's interests and how they should be aware of these when planning the curriculum. ■ Maier's students identified a range of facts about the Antarctic that they used to investigate their own questions about the geography and residents of Antarctica.

Meeting the standards is not the only concern of teachers, however. In a recent meeting with a group of 13 urban teachers Larson has been working with for eight years as part of a university/school literacy collaboration,[2] teachers articulated their concerns about 'new' literacies. As part of this work together, the group meets every summer for a week to read and discuss literacy research and theory, then develops plans to implement some of these ideas in the upcoming academic year. In the summer of 2004, the group read Lankshear and Knobel's (2003a) *New Literacies: Changing Knowledge and Classroom Learning* and developed a collaborative website.[3] The discussions focused on the arguments we discussed in Chapter 4 about the changing nature of literacy knowledge. The teachers realized some of their own assumptions about literacy and technology, and grew very concerned about what thinking about literacy like this would mean for their classrooms and their students. They recognized that their current thinking represented what Lankshear and Knobel (2003a) referred to as an outsider mindset. One 30-year veteran kindergarten teacher articulated what the teachers were worried about. Three main concerns emerged:

reading is disappearing;

the 'basics' of writing are losing value;

will all the 'old' be thrown out?

As a group, they all seemed to be worried about the role of correctness in the practice of literacies in general and 'new' literacies in particular. They worried that their students specifically would be further marginalized by not having access to the kinds of technology and practices needed and that their own lack of expertise was a serious block to such access.

One teacher expressed frustration that the NCLB model is so small and so restrictive that they have no choice but to do what is required and no time to look for something more meaningful. To him, meaning seems to have 'left the building'. All the teachers felt that so much has 'left the building': meaning, relevance, interest, hope. Even teachers. Many of their colleagues are choosing to leave the profession rather than conform to reductionist mandates.

As part of our discussion, the group went to different websites and noticed that there did not seem to be a lack of writing and that the writing itself was correct by academic standards. The teachers were talking about explicit teaching in skills of proper spelling and punctuation, stating that we need to teach traditional skills (for example, correct school-based literacy). None of these teachers want to teach literacy skills out of context and they do not believe, at least overtly, in an autonomous definition of literacy, but the fear they expressed was real nonetheless.

In the analysis of Internet texts, the group found that audience and purpose were not outmoded in a digital world. Text, however multimodal, has an audience and a purpose, and traditionally defined correctness will apply accordingly. The teachers connected these ideas to defining literacy as a social practice, asking 'What are people, including us, doing with literacy, digital or otherwise, in everyday and professional lives?' We came to realize that teachers need to become researchers of their own and their students' practices so they can make classrooms relevant spaces for learning. The group realized that they did indeed use multimodal and digital texts in their everyday lives and that understanding these practices and themselves as users of these texts will inform their teaching.

The teachers felt strongly that the consequences of not recognizing and using multimodal and digital texts on students were dire, especially for their urban students. They discussed that teacher educators already face an urban teaching force that operates hegemonically on a deficit model ideology (Irvine and Larson, 2001; James-Wilson, 2004; Larson and Irvine, 1999). Combine this deficit view with the restricted access to both hardware and practices typically experienced by underserved students, and they saw increased marginalization.

What tend to go unrecognized are the existing practices students bring to school that are multimodal and highly sophisticated technologically. Video-game play is a dominant practice for many children and young people, and the multimodal practices are similar to those discussed in Kress (2003), as Gee (2003) points out. However, the complex practices that are an integral part of video games are seldom embedded in schooled techno-literacy practices. Not only do students see school, therefore, as irrelevant, they feel unvalued and think that their 'ruling passions' (Barton and Hamilton, 1998) do not matter much. As Gee (2003) argues, even white middle-class children understand that school is irrelevant and teaches anachronistic skills and knowledge, it is just that they follow the 'rules' because the rules are made for them. The teachers in this group agreed that what mattered most to them was whether or not the teaching and learning of literacy are 'good', good in the sense of being meaningful, relevant and purposeful to those teaching and learning. Whether or not the literacies we use are chronologically 'old' is not the issue. As Colin Lankshear suggested in an email conversation with Larson about what constitutes 'new':

> A lot of what all of us use all the time is 'old' (in terms of chronology). But it is the inflection we give it that is important. I fall back on a lot of 'old' literacies all the time – but as much as possible with a view to achieving what I see as progressive ends that look as much to the future as to the past, and that look beyond cultural trappings of privilege, and beyond lowest common denominators of the 'popular' toward things I think are going to have principled purchase in the foreseeable future, and for ends I think are good and fair … In the final analysis, I think that a lot of savvy 'new literate kids' who understand 'code' and analysis and who think and be like Pearl Jam

will be important to the saving of this planet. But the campesinos will be by their side. The big fear I have is that 'the truly schooled' are the major threat to a plausible future. (Lankshear, 2004: personal communication)

The group of teachers involved in this network reflected on what it means to say a mode of literacy is 'new' and the same for other aspects of literacy education in a contemporary context. They wondered about what kind of society we would have if we constructed generations of rule-followers instead of authors? Lankshear and Knobel (2003a) and others seem to be arguing that no matter what schools are doing, children are making meaning and being productive on their own. Rogoff (1994) points out that learning happens in all contexts, it is the 'what' that changes. What is the 'what' we need to be teaching in today's context? Although there are thoughtful accounts of the kind of education schools should be providing now and in the future (Lankshear, forthcoming), this question is, perhaps, best addressed through the development of teacher-researcher networks, such as the one described above. Such networks offer opportunities for teachers to chew over ideas, share reflections and try out new curriculum and pedagogical approaches in a supportive context. We would suggest that some key features of such networks are:

- the involvement of teachers who have self-identified as co-inquirers into a particular issue/set of issues;

- the involvement of an academic who can work alongside the teachers and provide the kind of support which can be offered by someone who has a wide knowledge of research and publications in the field;

- the identification of an issue or set of issues that is of significant interest to all in the group;

- commitment to the trying out of ideas in the classroom, so that the outcomes can be reflected on in a critical manner in the network;

- a commitment to scholarly inquiry.[4]

As Lankshear and Knobel suggested in Chapter 3, research which involves teachers examing the out-of-school practices of learners is invaluable in forging an understanding of what children bring to the classroom and can help teachers to devise means of building on this in meaningful ways. However, we also feel that it is essential to conduct research that examines different curricula and pedagogical models closely and enables teachers to relate theory to practice in the classroom in dynamic ways. In-service teachers can obviously also benefit from more formal professional development models for which they attend courses and training days, but they also need opportunities to engage in the longitudinal processes that a research network can provide.

IMPLICATIONS FOR PRE-SERVICE TEACHERS

So far, we have considered the implications of the theoretical models offered in this book in terms of in-service teachers. However, it is also essential to consider the needs of pre-service teachers, given the constraints faced by institutions offering relevant courses. In this section of the chapter, we draw on research undertaken by Marsh (2003b), in which the experiences of pre-service teachers on a primary education course in England were tracked. The primary aim of the study was to determine the influences on pre-service teachers' construction of the literacy curriculum and the extent to which students were able to include media and popular cultural texts in their practice. This was felt to be important because of the developing understanding we have of the significance of building on children and young people's popular cultural practices in schools (Alvermann et al., 1999; Dyson, 2002; Marsh and Millard, 2000). Children are immersed in a world in which popular culture is linked to a growing number of leisure pursuits, if we view popular culture as practices shared by large groups of people and different in nature from 'high' culture (Jenks, 1993). However, it is also clear that children and young people develop popular cultural practices that are specific to local sites and, therefore, it is not possible to provide a definitive list of children's popular cultural interests. Nevertheless, it has been possible to determine the relationship between popular culture and schooling, and research in this area has enabled the following themes to be identified:

1 Popular culture can be motivational for young children and can be embedded into schooled literacy practices in meaningful ways (Dyson, 1994; 1998; 2000; 2001b; Marsh 1999; 2000a; 2000b; Pompe, 1996).

2 Popular culture can provide a forum in which dialogic communities can be constructed, particularly helpful for children for whom English is an additional language (Marsh, 2000a; Orellana, 1994).

3 Popular culture can provide a means of recognizing children's cultural capital in the literacy curriculum (Dyson, 2002; Marsh and Millard, 2000).

4 Children recontextualize and reconfigure their knowledge of popular cultural texts when creating new texts in the classroom (Belton, 2000; Dyson, 2001a; Robinson, 1997).

5 Popular cultural texts can provide a bridge between 'official' and 'unofficial' texts in school, for example, Greek gods and superheroes (Dyson, 1998).

6 Popular culture can provide a useful tool in the development of critical literacy skills (Alvermann et al., 1999; Comber and Simpson, 2001), as children already have well-developed critical skills in relation to a range of popular texts.

Because of the significance of some of these themes, Marsh felt that it was important to determine the extent to which pre-service teachers could draw on popular cultural texts in their construction of a literacy curriculum. In the first year of a three-year initial teacher education course in the UK, 118 students completed a questionnaire and 43 of this same group completed a follow-up questionnaire in the final year of the course. These questionnaires explored students' attitudes to and experiences of literacy, media and popular culture in educational contexts. Eighteen students volunteered to take part in group and individual interviews at various points throughout the course. These interviews explored in further detail some of the emergent themes from the questionnaires.

The data arising from the range of methods outlined previously enabled a map of influences on student teachers' construction of the curriculum to be traced over a four-year period (Figure 7.1).

In this model, there are seven factors that impact on the construction of the literacy curriculum. First is the prescribed curriculum itself. As this always frames the curriculum offered by pre- and in-service teachers, this is placed in the center of the diagram. Of course, the extent to which teachers challenge the content and structuring of the prescribed curriculum so that it is weakened or strengthened will vary, and will rely on the influence of the other six (A–F) factors. These six factors are: internal influences; external influences; subject knowledge; pedagogical content knowledge; sociocultural factors and structural factors. Inevitably, some of these factors overlap, for example, 'external influences' and 'sociocultural context'. In addition, it is often difficult to separate internal and external influences on the construction of the curriculum (Shulman and Shulman, 2004). Nevertheless, in the following section, each of these factors will be considered briefly in order to identify the key influences on the pre-service teachers' construction of the curriculum.

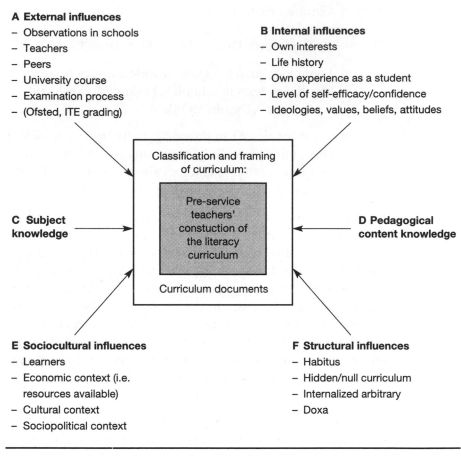

A External influences
- Observations in schools
- Teachers
- Peers
- University course
- Examination process
- (Ofsted, ITE grading)

B Internal influences
- Own interests
- Life history
- Own experience as a student
- Level of self-efficacy/confidence
- Ideologies, values, beliefs, attitudes

Classification and framing
of curriculum:

Pre-service
teachers'
constuction of
the literacy
curriculum

Curriculum documents

C Subject knowledge

D Pedagogical content knowledge

E Sociocultural influences
- Learners
- Economic context (i.e. resources available)
- Cultural context
- Sociopolitical context

F Structural influences
- Habitus
- Hidden/null curriculum
- Internalized arbitrary
- Doxa

Figure 7.1 Influences on pre-service teachers' construction of the literacy curriculum

FACTOR A: EXTERNAL INFLUENCES

Factor A outlines a range of external influences on the pre-service teachers' construction of the curriculum, all identified as salient issues by the students taking part in this study. These include observations undertaken in schools (McIntyre et al., 1996); influence of teachers and peers (Carter and Doyle, 1996); impact of the initial teacher education (ITE) curriculum (Patrick-Diamond, 1991); and the influence of normalizing factors (Foucault, 1977) such as school inspections and various types of examinations (in this case, the grading system for gaining qualified teacher status [QTS]). Students mentioned all these factors as important in limiting the extent to which they felt they could introduce more 'adventurous' approaches to the teaching of literacy on their placements.

▨ FACTOR B: INTERNAL INFLUENCES

Factor B indicates the range of internal influences on the pre-service students' practices. There is research that indicates that beliefs and attitudes are two of the strongest internal factors on teachers' practice (Clandinin, 1986; Nespor, 1987; Pajares, 1992). A number of studies have indicated that pre-service teachers hold rather conservative views with regard to the curriculum and pedagogy (Civil, 1993; McDiarmid, 1990). This was certainly the case with regard to this group of students' conception of the English curriculum, as throughout their course, they consistently privileged traditional approaches to grammar and phonics in their teaching placements. A second, strong factor in relation to internal influences was students' life-history experiences, as indicated in previous research (Britzman, 1989; Grossman, 1990; Lortie, 1975). The majority of students did not use popular culture or media in any of their teaching placements and many suggested that one of the factors was lack of experiences of these texts in their own school experience.

▨ FACTORS C AND D: SUBJECT KNOWLEDGE AND PEDAGOGICAL CONTENT KNOWLEDGE

Subject knowledge has been identified as an important element of teachers' construction of the curriculum (Grossman, 1990; Medwell et al., 1998) and is represented in Factor C. In relation to this study, lack of knowledge about popular culture appeared to inhibit a number of students' use of such texts in the curriculum. Factor D represents pedagogical content knowledge (Shulman, 1987). Pedagogical content knowledge refers to the knowledge needed in order to teach the content of a particular subject. Students consistently stated that they needed guidance in relation to pedagogical content knowledge when using popular culture in the literacy curriculum. Therefore, it was clear that these two factors were important in limiting the extent to which the students felt they could challenge the given curriculum. However, teachers' subject knowledge is, inevitably, shaped by sociocultural discourses that influence what is considered to be appropriate or not within an educational domain, as the next factor indicates.

▨ FACTOR E: SOCIOCULTURAL INFLUENCES

Factor E outlines all the features of the sociocultural context in which teachers operate. Central to this context are the learners themselves, whose characteristics, interests and abilities will affect the construction of the curriculum (Ross, 2003). Economic and cultural factors also shape teacher decision-making, and sociopolitical contexts inevitably impact on the construction of the curriculum. For instance, computer games have been at the center of widespread moral panics in the media about young children and violence in contemporary society and, in this study, the student teachers' revoiced some of the concerns raised when dismissing this genre as a useful educational tool.

■ FACTOR F: STRUCTURAL INFLUENCES

Factor F outlines those structural features that were seen throughout this study to have influenced the construction of the curriculum. The habitus[5] (Bourdieu, 1990) developed by experiences in the primary schools influences the curriculum through shaping what is *not* taught, the hidden or null curriculum (Britzman, 1989; Eisner, 1979), in addition to what is taught. Bourdieu's concept of doxa is also pertinent here. Doxa 'is the relationship of immediate adherence that is established in practice between a habitus and the field to which it is attuned, the pre-verbal taking-for-granted of the world that flows from practical sense' (Bourdieu, 1990: 68). As Webb et al. point out: 'Doxa works to distinguish the thinkable from the unthinkable, so that certain courses of action, those that seriously challenge established social relations, become literally unthinkable – or at least, inarticulable' (2002: 119).

In the case of the students in this study, their habitus was perfectly attuned to the field of literacy education as constituted in schools. Popular culture, therefore, became the 'unthinkable' and its use in the curriculum simply not considered most of the time. Their ideas about literacy practices connect saliently to those articulated by the in-service teachers who work with Larson. To the latter, multimodal literacies and popular culture were as yet unthinkable resources for the curriculum.

In relation to the discussion in this book, Figure 7.1 presents a useful tool for beginning to think about how initial teacher education programs could ensure that students have access to theoretical models of literacy that move beyond the confines of mandated curricula. In particular, Factors C and D would indicate that student teachers should have sufficient knowledge about alternative models in order that they can begin to plan curricula that incorporate aspects of NLS, techno-literacy, critical literacy or sociocultural-historical theory. This may be difficult in a context in which there is much pressure on program time, but necessary if students are to feel sufficiently knowledgeable to challenge normative models of literacy. Given the way in which some of the other factors militate against the development of non-normative models, due to the pervasive influence of biographical experiences or school cultures for example, it is even more important that pre-service courses provide alternative models that can be drawn upon when necessary. Pre-service teachers should, therefore, have more extensive opportunities to explore various conceptions of literacy in order to ensure that they do not locate their practice solely within an autonomous (Street, 1984) model. In particular, students should have opportunities to explore the matches and mismatches between children' out-of-school literacy practices and those they encounter in the school curriculum (Brooker, 2002; Gregory and Williams, 2000).

In addition, it would be useful for pre-service teachers to be able to consider some of the influences on their construction of the literacy curriculum in a structured way. Indeed, Figure 7.1 could be used as a heuristic device for deconstructing students' experiences and allowing them to trace how these different factors impact on it, thus providing opportunities for them to identify ways in which hegemonic models could be challenged.

Student teachers also need access to resources that would enable them to draw on various theoretical models within their literacy curriculum, for example, relevant research papers, textbooks and teaching materials that draw on these theoretical frameworks. It was clear from the study outlined briefly here that such material is rarely available in primary schools and, thus, it is even more important that higher education institutions offer the broadest range of resources possible. Ultimately, what we are arguing here is that a crucial area of focus for all educators interested in broadening normative conceptions of literacy should be the education of pre-service teachers, for it is there that opportunities for the future lie and it is there that potential for change can be seen. If we are to develop literacy curricula that reflect the realities of children's out-of-school literacy lives, embedded as they are in technological discourses and media and popular cultural texts, then it is incumbent upon teacher educators to ensure that pre- and in-service teachers are aware of the issues and are able to respond sensitively to children's needs.

Despite extensive limitations, many teachers are able to offer creative and challenging literacy curricula that challenge autonomous models of literacy and, indeed, the case studies in this book attest to this fact. But this work is undertaken in spite of mandated policy, not because of it. There need to be widespread policy changes if more teachers are able to undertake the kind of work outlined in these pages. We suggest three here. First, national and state literacy curricula need to provide sufficient space for teachers to draw from a range of theoretical models as they plan their classroom practice, and not force teachers into a subversive space that has negative career consequences. Highly restrictive models, with strong classification and framing (Bernstein, 1974), as discussed in Chapter 1, should be resisted. Second, teacher education programmes need to be able to provide an expansive exploration of various models of literacy in order that students can make informed choices about their classroom practice. Finally, in-service professional development should offer opportunities for teachers to engage in action research projects in which they can explore various theoretical models and examine how theory interrelates with practice. Larson's long-term relationship with teachers in one building is one example of the kind of relationships that may facilitate teachers' theoretical understandings.[6]

So far in this chapter, we have considered the implication of the theoretical frameworks outlined in this book for in-service and pre-service teachers' practice, in addition to policy. In the final section of this chapter, we move on to consider the implications for research.

IMPLICATIONS FOR RESEARCH

Although there are a growing number of accounts of the relationship between the various theoretical models of literacy discussed in this book and classroom practice (Street, forthcoming), this is obviously an area for continued focus. In addition, there need to be further studies that explore the integration of the different models and the implications for curriculum and pedagogy. For example, what does critical literacy look like in relation to online texts? What practices are carried across the different modes and media, and what is different? In what ways have textual audiences and purposes changed? These questions have barely begun to be addressed in the literature focusing on literacy and new technologies, and there are similar questions that should be addressed in relation to the convergence of other theoretical models.

In addition, literacy research also needs to continue to explore the relationship between literacy practices undertaken in different domains. Whilst some argue that the home–school border is crossed in a number of subtle and important ways (Street, forthcoming), others suggest that these crossings are shaped by the hegemonic forces of schooled literacy practices; the direction of travel is thus rather one-way (Marsh, 2003a). This is an area which needs more careful attention. What happens when children's out-of-school practices travel into the classroom? How do schooled literacy practices permeate out-of-school contexts, and what are the consequences for 'vernacular literacy' (Barton and Hamilton, 1998)? These questions relate to the convergence of space, time and literacy, which also needs further consideration. Sheehy and Leander have pointed to the way in which: 'Our metaphorical spatial lexic matters, and tracing how it matters inevitably leads us to "matter" in the world, to the material stuff of our home lives and cityscapes, which absorbs us and which we continually interpret through the word' (2004: 3). Exploring the way in which literacy practices construct spaces and those spaces inform literacy practices is a current concern of a number of literacy researchers (Comber et al., 2001; Davies, forthcoming; Leander and Sheehy, 2004; Marsh, forthcoming; Pahl, 2005) and further work is needed to incorporate this understanding into pedagogical practice.

Finally, the implications for future research of some of the work embedded in the case studies featured in this book are significant. How can teachers carve out the time and space for continued critical reflection, which is essential in the development of praxis? How do teachers' professional identities relate to their continued commitment to scholarly enquiry, and how can this be supported by working alongside colleagues and academic co-researchers? There needs to be further research that sheds light on some of these processes and informs the development of meaningful and challenging contexts for professional learning. As Lankshear and Knobel suggest in their interview in Chapter 4, we need also to value research that is trying to understand new phenomena, practices and meanings, and not immediately jump to making connections to practice. We restate our argument from Chapter 1: theory is practice and practice is theory.

CONCLUSION

In this book, we have outlined four theories of literacy in an attempt to facilitate discussions about literacy learning and pedagogy. The case studies have provided glimpses into the practices of teachers who draw from these theories in the construction of their curriculum and shaping of their pedagogy, in order to offer concrete examples of these theories embedded in meaningful practice. In addition, the reflections of key theorists in each of these areas have helped to crystallize the basic principles of each of the models and have been important in identifying possible future directions in terms of research, policy and practice. We have made several key arguments throughout these chapters, but would like to close by emphasizing just four.

First, theory counts. All teachers and researchers have theories of language and literacy and of learning. These theories frame research and pedagogy. Theories can be aligned with traditional definitions of literacy, or they can contest these definitions. We claim here that contesting these definitions is preferable to maintaining the status quo, given the changing nature of literacy in an information and communication economy, and the need to provide suitable educational experiences for the future generation of 'shape shifting portfolio people' that Gee (2004) talks about. Second, we argue that a multidisciplinary theory of literacy learning values the experiences and knowledge that children bring to the classroom. Students count. Complex theories of literacy, as outlined here, have the potential to counteract the deficit model by challenging conceptions of children's language and literacy practices in terms of what they lack compared to school literacy. Third, we argue that educators need to do more than 'link' home and school literacies. We need to move beyond simply valuing or celebrating students' literacies, but actively and meaningfully use these literacies in the curriculum. Recent work in new literacies argues that literacy does more than bridge or connect home and school. Literacies are spacialized (Leander and Sheehy, 2004) and as such travel across time and space as people use them. Students should not have to choose between one domain or another. They should be able to make sense of their lives with literacy across contexts. Teachers thus need to avoid pedagogizing out-of-school literacies or just simply repackaging them in a school-based framework, instead they need to provide spaces for students to consider aspects of their literacy lives in a range of contexts and for them to make meaningful connections across these spaces. Finally, we suggest that the kinds of educational opportunities that are outlined in this book can be offered more widely if educators, researchers and policy-makers are willing to reflect in critical ways on current practice and are prepared to take risks. Not to do so would be to ensure that literacy education in the twenty-first century continues to reproduce literacy pedagogy from the eighteenth century.

NOTES

1 http://www.emsc.nysed.gov/3-8/elaverview.htm

2 Larson has been working with teachers in a literacy professional development project funded by the New York State Department of Education. All but one of the 13 teachers currently in the project teach at School 28 in the Rochester City School District, the same school where Lynn Gatto teaches (see Chapter 2). The remaining teacher comes to each meeting from a neighboring suburb. The group meets monthly throughout the academic year and for a week each summer.

3 http://www.rochester.edu/Warner/researchprojects/collaborative/index.html

4 It is beyond the scope of this chapter to outline what constitutes quality professional development. See Darling-Hammond (1994) and Darling-Hammond and Sykes (1999) for discussion of this literature.

5 Bourdieu (1990) defines habitus as a person's beliefs, dispositions, and practices that make up his/her ideational world, including body movements and postures, social structures, thought and knowledge. The idea of habitus connects to Gee's (1996) definitions of D/discourse as ways of viewing, interpreting and acting in the world.

6 See Note 2.

References

Alvermann, D., Moon, J.S. and Hagood, M.C. (1999) *Popular Culture in the Classroom: Teaching and Researching Critical Media Literacy*. Newark, DE: IRA/NRC.

Anderson, G. and Irvine, P. (1993) Informing critical literacy with ethnography, in C. Lankshear and P. McLaren (eds), *Critical Literacy: Politics, Praxis, and the Postmodern*. Albany, NY: SUNY Press.

Atwell, N. (1998) *In the Middle: New Understandings about Writing, Reading, and learning*. 2nd edn. Portsmouth, NH: Heinemann.

Bakhtin, M.M. (1981) *The Dialogic Imagination*. Ed. M. Holquist. Trans M. Holquist and C. Emerson. Austin, TX: University of Texas Press.

Bakhtin, M.M. (1986) *Speech Genres and Other Late Essays*. Austin, TX: University of Texas Press.

Ball, A. (1995) Text design patterns in the writing of urban African American students: teaching to the cultural strengths of students in multicultural settings, *Urban Education*, 30(3): 253–89.

Barton, D. (1994) *Literacy: An Introduction to the Ecology of Written Language*. Oxford: Blackwell.

Barton, D. and Hamilton, M. (1998) *Local Literacies*. London: Routledge.

Belton, T. (2000) Reading between the lines of children's stories, *Educational Research*, 42(3): 251–60.

Berger, A.A. (2000) Arthur's computer (narrative) adventure, *TelevIZIon*, 13(1): 40.

Berger, P. and Luckman, T. (1966) *The Social Construction of Reality: A Treatise in the Sociology of Knowledge*. Garden City, NY: Doubleday.

Bernstein, B. (1974) *Class, Codes and Control*. Vol. 1. 2nd edn. London: Routledge and Kegan Paul.

Bernstein, B. (1977) Class and pedagogies: visible and invisible, in J. Karabel and A.H. Halsey (eds), *Power and Ideology in Education*. New York: Oxford University Press.

Bernstein, B. (1996) *Pedagogy, Symbolic Control and Identity: Theory, Research, Critique*. London: Taylor and Francis.

Bernstein, B. (2000) *Pedagogy, Symbolic Control and Identity: Theory, Research, Critique*. Revd edn. London: Taylor and Francis.

Bigum, C. (2002) Design sensibilities, schools, and the new computing and communications technologies, in I. Snyder (ed.), *Silicon Literacies*. London: RoutledgeFalmer.

Bigum, C. (2003) The knowledge producing school: moving away from finding educational problems for which computers are solutions. At http://www.deakin.edu.au/education/lit/kps/pubs/comp_in_nz.rtf.

Bloome, D., Carter, S., Christian, B., Otto, S. and Shuart-Faris, N. (2005) *Discourse Analysis and the Study of Classroom Language and Literacy Events: A Microanalytic Perspective*. Mahwah, NJ: Lawrence Erlbaum Associates.

Bourdieu, P. (1990) *The Logic of Practice*. Trans. R. Nice. Cambridge: Polity Press (Original work published in 1980.)

Bourdieu, P. and Passeron, J.C. (1977) *Reproduction in Education, Society and Culture*. London: Sage.

Brady, J. and Hernández, A. (1993) Feminist literacies: toward emancipatory possibilities of solidarity, in C. Lankshear and P. McLaren (eds), *Critical Literacy: Politics, Praxis, and the Postmodern*. Albany, NY: SUNY Press.

Bredekamp, S. (1987) *Developmentally Appropriate Practice in Early Childhood Programs Serving Children from Birth through Age Eight*. Washington, DC: NAEYC.

Britzman, D.P. (1989) Who has the floor? Curriculum, teaching and the English student teachers' struggle for voice, *Curriculum Inquiry*, 19(2): 143–62.

Brooker, L. (2002) *Starting School: Young Children Learning Cultures*. Buckingham: Open University Press.

Bruner, J. (1975) From communication to language: A psychological perspective, *Cognition*, 3: 255–87.

Buckingham, D. (2003) *Media Education: Literacy, Learning and Contemporary Culture*. Oxford: Polity Press.

Burn, A. and Leach, J. (2004) ICTs and moving image literacy in English, in R. Andrews (ed.), *The Impact of ICTs on English 5–16*. pp. 153–79. London: RoutledgeFalmer.

Burnett, C., Dickinson, P., Malden, H., Merchant, G. and Myers, J. (2004) Digital connections: purposeful uses of email in the primary school, paper presented at United Kingdom Literacy Association's (UKLA) Annual Conference, Manchester.

Calkins, L. (1994) *The Art of Teaching Writing*. New edn. Portsmouth, NH: Heinemann.

Carrington, V. (2004) Texts and literacies of the Shi Jinrui, *British Journal of Sociology of Education*, 25(2): 215–28.

Carrington, V. and Luke, A. (2003) Reading, home and families: from post-modern to modern? in A. van Kleek, S.A.Stahl and E.B. Bauer (eds), *On Reading to Children: Parents and Teachers*. Mahwah, NJ: Lawrence Erlbaum Associates.

Carter, K. and Doyle, W. (1996) Personal narrative and life history in learning to teach, in J. Sikula, T.J. Buttery and E. Guyton (eds), *Handbook of Research on Teacher Education*. New York: Simon and Schuster/Macmillan.

Cazden, C. (1988) *Classroom Discourse: The Language of Teaching and Learning*. Portsmouth, NH: Heinemann.

Certeau, M. de (1984) *The Practice of Everyday Life*. Berkeley, CA: University of California Press.

Civil, M. (1993) Prospective elementary teachers' thinking about teaching mathematics, *Journal of Mathematics Behaviour*, 12(1): 79–109.

Clandinin, D.J. (1986) *Classroom Practice: Teacher Images in Action*. London: Falmer Press.

Cole, M. (1996) *Cultural Psychology: A Once and Future Discipline*. Cambridge, MA: Harvard University Press.

Cole, M. and Engeström, Y. (1993) A cultural-historical approach to distributed cognition, in G. Salomon (ed.), *Distributed Cognitions: Psychological and Educational Considerations*. pp. 1–46. New York: Cambridge University Press.

Comber, B. (1993) Classroom explorations in critical literacy, *Australian Journal of Language and Literacy*, 16(1): 73–83.

Comber, B. (1994) Critical literacy: an introduction to Australian debates and perspectives, *Journal of Curriculum Studies*, 26(6): 655–68.

Comber, B. (2001a) Critical literacy and local action: teacher knowledge and a 'new' research agenda, in B. Comber and A. Simpson (eds), *Negotiating Critical Literacies in Classrooms*. pp. 271–82. Mahwah, NJ, and London: Lawrence Erlbaum Associates.

Comber, B. (2001b) Negotiating critical literacies, *School Talk*, 6(3): 1–2.

Comber, B. (2003) Critical literacy in the Early Years: What does it look like? in N. Hall, J. Larson and J. Marsh (eds), *Handbook of Early Childhood Literacy*. London: Sage.

Comber, B. and Nixon, H. (2004) Children re-read and re-write their local neighbourhoods: critical literacies and identity work, in J. Evans (ed.), *Literacy Moves On*. pp. 115–32. London: David Fulton; Portsmouth, NH: Heinemann.

Comber, B. and Simpson, A. (1995) Reading cereal boxes, *Texts: The Heart of the English Curriculum*. Adelaide: Department for Education and Children's Services.

Comber, B. and Simpson (eds) (2001) *Negotiating Critical Literacies in Classrooms*. Mahwah, NJ, and London: Lawrence Erlbaum Associates.

Comber, B. Thomson, P., with Wells, M. (2001) Critical literacy finds a 'place': writing and social action in a neighborhood school, *Elementary School Journal*, 101(4): 451–64.

Cope, B. and Kalantzis, M. (1993) *The Powers of Literacy: A Genre Approach to the Teaching of Writing*. London: Falmer Press.

Cope, B. and Kalantzis, M (eds) (2000) *Multiliteracies: Literacy Learning and the Design of Social Futures*. London: Routledge.

Daiute, C. (1993) The development of literacy through social interaction, *New Directions for Child Development*, no. 61. San Francisco: Jossey-Bass.

Darling-Hammond, L. (1994) *Professional Development Schools: Schools for Developing a Profession*. New York: Teachers College Press.

Darling-Hammond, L. and Sykes, G. (eds) (1999) *Teaching as the Learning Profession: Handbook of Policy and Practice*. San Francisco: Jossey-Bass.

Davidson, C.R. (2005) The social organization of independent writing in an early years classroom, unpublished PhD dissertation, University of Queensland, Australia.

Davies, J. (forthcoming) Nomads and tribes: On-line meaning making and the development of new literacies, in J. Marsh and E. Millard (eds), *Popular Literacies, Childhood and Schooling*. London: RoutledgeFalmer.

Dawes, L. and Dumbleton, T. (2001) Computer games in education project, BECTA. At http://www.becta.org.uk/page_documents/research/cge/report.pdf.

Department for Education and Employment (DfEE) (1998) *National Literacy Strategy: Framework for Teaching*. London: HMSO.

Department for Education and Employment (DfEE)/Qualifications and Curriculum Authority (QCA) (1999) *The National Curriculum*. London: HMSO.

Department for Education and Skills (DfES) (1999) *Progression in Phonics*. London: HMSO.

Dewey, J. (1938) *Logic: The Theory of Inquiry*. New York: Holt and Co.

Duranti, A. (1997) *Linguistic Anthropology*. Cambridge: Cambridge University Press.

Dyson, A. (1993) *Social Worlds of Children Learning to Write in an Urban Primary School*. New York: Teachers College Press.

Dyson, A.H. (1994) The Ninjas, the X-men, and the ladies: playing with power and identity in an urban primary school, *Teachers College Record*, 96(2): 219–39.

Dyson, A. (1997) *Writing Superheroes: Contemporary Childhood, Popular Culture, and Classroom Literacy*. New York: Teachers College Press.

Dyson, A.H. (1998) Folk processes and media creatures: reflections on popular culture for literacy educators, *The Reading Teacher*, 51(5): 392–402.

Dyson, A.H. (1999) Transforming transfer: unruly children, contrary texts and the persistence of the pedagogical order, in A. Iran-Nejad and P.D Pearson (eds), *Review of Research in Education*, 24. Washington, DC: American Educational Research Association, pp. 9–39.

Dyson, A.H. (2000) On reframing children's words: the perils, promises, and pleasures of writing children, *Research in the Teaching of English*, 34(3): 352–67.

Dyson, A. (2001a) Where are the childhoods in childhood literacy? An exploration in outer (school) space, *Journal of Early Childhood Literacy*, 1(1): 9–39.

Dyson, A.H. (2001b) Donkey Kong in Little Bear country: a first-grader's composing development in the media spotlight, *Elementary School Journal*, 101(4): 417–33.

Dyson, A.H. (2002) *Brothers and Sisters Learn to Write: Popular Literacies in Childhood and School Cultures*. New York: Teachers College Press.

Edelsky, C. (1991) *With Literacy and Justice for All: Rethinking The Social In Language and Education*. New York: Falmer.

Education Queensland (2000) *Why Wait? A Way into Teaching Critical Literacies in the Early Years*. Brisbane: The State of Queensland, Department of Education.

Egan-Robertson, A. and Bloome, D. (eds) (1998) *Students as Researchers of Culture and Language in Their Own Communities*. Cresskill, NJ: Hampton.

Ehri, L.C. (1987) Learning to read and spell words, *Journal of Reading Behaviour*, 19: 5–31.

Ehri, L.C. (1995) Phases of development in learning to read words by sight, *Journal of Research in Reading*, 18(2): 116–25.

Eisner, E. (1979) *The Educational Imagination*. New York: Macmillan.

Elkind, D. (1981) *The Hurried Child*. Reading, MA: Addison-Wesley.

Elsasser, N. and Irvine, P.D. (1985) English and creole: the dialectics of choice in a college writing program, *Harvard Educational Review*, 55: 399–415.

Enciso, P. (2005) Reframing history in sociocultural theory: toward an expansive vision, in C. Lewis, P. Enciso and E. Moje (eds), *Reframing Sociocultural Theory and Research*. Mahwah, NJ: Lawrence Erlbaum Associates.

Erickson, F. (1986) Qualitative methods in research on teaching, in M. Wittrock (ed.), *Handbook of Research on Teaching*. pp. 119–61. Washington, DC: AERA.

Erickson, F. (1996) Going for the zone: the social and cognitive ecology of teacher–student interaction in classroom conversations, in D. Hicks (ed.), *Discourse, Learning, and Schooling*. pp. 29–62. Cambridge: Cambridge University Press.

Everett, A. (2003) Digitextuality and click theory: theses on convergence media in the digital age, in A. Everett and J.T. Caldwell (eds), *New Media: Theories and Practices of Digitextuality*. New York: Routledge.

Facer, K., Sutherland, R., Furlong, R. and Furlong, J. (2003) *Screen Play: Children and Computers in the Home*. London: RoutledgeFalmer.

Fairclough, N. (1992) *Discourse and Social Change*. Cambridge: Polity Press.

Foucault, M. (1972) *The Archaeology of Knowledge*. Trans. A. Sheridan Smith. Oxford: Basil Blackwell.

Foucault, M. (1977) *Discipline and Punish: The Birth of the Prison*. Harmondsworth: Penguin.

Fountas, G.S. and Pinnell, I. (1996) *Guided Reading: Good First Teaching for All Children*. Portsmouth, NH: Heinemann.

Freebody, P. and Luke, A. (1990) Literacies programs: debates and demands in cultural context, *Prospect: Australian Journal of TESOL*, 5(3): 7–16.

Freebody, P. and Luke, A. (2003) Literacy as engaging with new forms of life: the 'four roles' model, in G. Bull and M. Anstey (eds), *The Literacy Lexicon*. 2nd edn. pp. 52–7. Sydney: Prentice Hall.

Freire, P. (1972) *Pedagogy of the Oppressed*. Trans. M. Bergman Ramos. London: Sheed and Ward.

Freire, P. (1989) *Pedagogy of the Oppressed*. New York: Continuum.

Freire, P. and Macedo, D. (1987) *Literacy: Reading the Word and the World*. London: Bergin and Garvey.

Gagnon, D. (1985) Videogames and spatial skills: an exploratory study, *Educational Communication and Technology Journal*, 33(4): 263–75.

Gallas, K. (1994) *The Languages of Learning: How Children Talk, Write, Dance, Draw, and Sing their Understanding of the World*. New York: Teachers College Press.

Gatto, L. (2001) Success guaranteed literacy programs: I don't buy it! In J. Larson (ed.), *Literacy as Snake Oil: Beyond the Quick Fix*. pp. 71–88. New York: Lang.

Gee, J.P. (1996) *Sociolinguistics and Literacies: Ideology in Discourses*. 2nd edn. London: Taylor and Francis.

Gee, J.P. (1999) *An Introduction to Discourse Analysis: Theory and Method*. New York: Routledge.

Gee, J.P. (2001) Reading, languages abilities, and semiotic resources: beyond limited perspectives on reading, in J. Larson (ed.), *Literacy as Snake Oil: Beyond the Quick Fix*. pp. 7–26. New York: Lang.

Gee, J.P. (2003) *What Video Games Have to Teach Us about Learning and Literacy*. New York: Palgrave Macmillan.

Gee, J.P. (2004) *Situated Language and Learning: A Critique of Traditional Schooling*. New York: Routledge.

Gee, J.P., Hull, G. and Lankshear, C. (1996) *The New Work Order: Behind the Language of the New Capitalism*. Sydney: Allen and Unwin.

Geertz, C. (1995) *After the Fact: Two Countries, Four Decades, One Anthropologist*. Cambridge, MA: Harvard University Press.

Gesell, A. (1940) *The First Five Years of Life*. New York: Harper and Row.

Giroux, H.A.(1988) *Schooling for Democracy: Critical Pedagogy in the Modern Age*. London: Routledge.

Glister, P. (1997) *Digital Literacy*. New York: John Wiley and Sons.

Goodwin, M. (1990) *He-said-she-said: Talk as Social Organization among Black Children*. Indianapolis, IN: Indiana University Press.

Gore, J.M. (1992) What we can do for you! What can 'W' do for 'You'?: Struggling over empowerment in critical and feminist pedagogy, in C. Luke and J. Gore (eds), *Feminisms and Critical Pedagogy*. pp. 54–73. New York: Routledge.

Gore, J.M. (1993) *The Struggle for Pedagogies: Critical and Feminist Discourses as Regimes of Truth*. New York: Routledge.

Graff, H. (1979) *The Literacy Myth: Literacy and Social Structures in the Nineteenth Century City*. New York: Academic Press.

Graves, D. (1983) *Writing: Teachers and Children at Work*. Portsmouth, NH: Heinemann.

Green, J. and J. Harker (eds) (1988) *Multiple Perspective Analysis of Classroom Discourse*. Norwood, NJ: Ablex.

Greenfield, P.M. (1984) *Mind and Media: The Effects of Television, Computers and Video Games*. London: Fontana.

Greenfield, P.M. and Cocking, R.R. (1994) Effects of interactive entertainment technologies on development, *Journal of Applied Developmental Psychology*, 15: 1–2.

Greenhough, P., Scanlan, M., Feiler, A., Johnson, D., Yee, W.C., Andrews, J., Price, A., Smithson, M. and Hughes, M. (forthcoming) Boxing clever: using shoeboxes to support home school knowledge exchange, *Literacy*.

Gregory, E. and Williams, A. (2000) *City Literacies: Learning to Read across Generations and Cultures*. London: Routledge.

Griffin, P. and Cole, M. (1984) Current activity for the future: the zo-ped, in B. Rogoff and J. Wertsch (eds), *Children's Learning in the Zone of Proximal Development*. pp. 45–64. New Directions for Child Development, no. 23. San Francisco: Jossey-Bass.

Grossman, P. (1990) *The Making of a Teacher: Teacher Knowledge and Teacher Education*. New York: Teachers College Press.

Gutierrez, K. (1993) How talk, context, and script shape contexts for learning: a cross-case comparison of journal sharing, *Linguistics and Education*, 5: 335–65.

Gutierrez, K. (2002) Studying cultural practices in urban learning communities, *Human Development*, 45(4): 312–21.

Gutierrez, K. and Rogoff, B. (2003) Cultural ways of learning: individual traits or repertoires of practice, *Educational Researcher*, 32(5): 19–25.

Gutierrez, K. and Stone, L. (2002) Hypermediating literacy activity: how learning contexts get reorganized, in O. Saracho and B. Spodek (eds), *Contemporary Perspectives in Early Childhood Education*. Vol. 2. pp. 25–51. Greenwich, CT: Information Age Publishing.

Hall, K. (2003) Effective literacy teaching in the early years of school: a review of the evidence, in N. Hall, J. Larson and J. Marsh (eds), *Handbook of Early Childhood Literacy*. London: Sage.

Hayward, B., Alty, C., Pearson, S. and Martin, C. (2003) *Young People and ICT 2002*. London: DfES/BECTA.

Heath, S.B. (1983) *Ways with Words: Language, Life, and Work in Communities and Classrooms*. Cambridge: Cambridge University Press.

Hill, S., Comber, B., Badger, L. and Nixon, H. (1994) *Literacy, Diversity and Schooling*. A three module video documentary and guide booklet, CAUT, University of South Australia, Eleanor Curtain Publishing, Melbourne (distributed by Heinemann, Portsmouth, NH, USA).

Holloway, S. and Valentine, G. (2003) *Cyberkids – Children in the New Information Age*. London: Routledge.

Hull, G. and Schultz, K. (2002) *School's Out! Bridging Out-of-school Literacies with Classroom Practice*. New York: Teachers College Press.

Irvine, P.D. and Elsasser, N. (1988) The ecology of literacy: negotiating writing standards in a Caribbean setting, in G. Rafoth and D. Rubin (eds), *The Social Construction of Written Language*. Norwood, NJ: Ablex.

Irvine, P.D. and Larson, J. (2001) Literacy packages in practice: constructing academic disadvantage, in J. Larson (ed.), *Literacy as Snake Oil: Beyond the Quick Fix*. pp. 45–70. New York: Lang.

James-Wilson, S.V. (2004) Towards a knowledge base for the preparation of urban and inner-city teachers: a social justice approach, unpublished doctoral dissertation, Toronto: University of Toronto.

Janks, H. (2000) Domination, access, diversity and design: a synthesis for critical literacy education, *Educational Review*, 52(2): 175–86.

Janks, H. and Comber, B. (2005) Critical literacy across continents, in K. Pahl and J. Rowsell (eds), *Travel Notes from the New Literacy Studies: Case Studies in Practice*. Clevedon: Multilingual Matters.

Jenks, C. (1993) *Culture*. London: Routledge.

Kamler, B. (2001) *Relocating the Personal: A Critical Writing Pedagogy*. Albany, NY: SUNY Press.

Kirriemuir, J. and McFarlane, A. (2004) *Literature review in games and learning*. NestaFuturelab.

Knobel, M. and Lankshear, C. (2003) The out-of-school literacy practices of children, in N. Hall, J. Larson and J. Marsh (eds), *Handbook of Early Childhood Literacy*. London, New Delhi and Thousand Oaks, CA: Sage.

Kraidy, M. (1999) The global, the local, and the hybrid: a native ethnography of glocalization, *Critical Studies in Mass Communication*, 16: 456–76.

Kress, G. (1997) *Before Writing*. London: Routledge

Kress, G. (2003) *Literacy in the New Media Age*. London: Routledge.

Ladson-Billings, G. (1994) *The Dreamkeepers: Successful Teachers of African American Children*. San Francisco, CA: Jossey-Bass.

Lankshear, C., with Gee, J.P., Knobel, M. and Searle, C. (1997) *Changing Literacies*. Buckingham: Open University Press.

Lankshear, C. (forthcoming) No single divide: literacies, new technologies and school-defined vs self-selected purposes in curriculum and pedagogy, in J. Marsh and E. Millard (eds), *Popular Literacies, Childhood and Schooling*. London: RoutledgeFalmer.

Lankshear, C. and Bigum, C. (1999) Literacies and new technologies in school settings, *Pedagogy, Culture and Society* (formerly *Curriculum Studies*), 7(3): 241–61.

Lankshear, C. and Knobel, C. (2003a) *New Literacies: Changing Knowledge and Classroom Learning*. Buckingham: Open University Press.

Lankshear, C. and Knobel, M. (2003b) Do-it-yourself broadcasting: writing weblogs in a knowledge society, paper presented to the Annual Meeting of the American Education Research Association, Chicago, IL, April.

Lankshear, C. and Knobel, M. (2004a) Planning pedagogy for i-mode: some principles for pedagogical decision-making, paper presented at the Annual Meeting of the American Education Research Association, San Diego, CA, April.

Lankshear, C. and Knobel, M. (2004b) Planning pedagogy for i-mode: from flogging to blogging via wi-fi, published jointly in *English in Australia*, 139 (February) and *Literacy Learning in the Middle Years*, 12(1): 78–102.

Lankshear, C. and Knobel, M. (2004c) Text-related roles of the digitally 'at home', paper presented at the American Education Research Association Annual Meeting, San Diego, CA, April.

Lankshear, C. and Knobel, M. (2004d) *A Handbook for Teacher Research*. Maidenhead and Philadelphia, PA: Open University Press.

Larson, J. (ed.) (2001) *Literacy as Snake Oil: Beyond the Quick Fix*. New York: Lang.

Larson, J. (2003) Negotiating race in classroom research: tensions and possibilities, in S. Greene and D. Abt-Perkins (eds), *Making Race Visible: Literacy Research for Cultural Understanding*. pp. 89–106. New York: Teachers College Press.

Larson, J. (2005) Breaching the classroom walls: literacy learning across time and space in an elementary school in the United States, in B. Street (ed.), *Literacies across Educational Contexts: Mediating Learning and Teaching*. pp. 84–101. Philadelphia, PA: Caslon Press.

Larson, J. and Gatto, L. (2004) Tactical underlife: understanding students' perspectives, *Journal of Early Childhood Literacy*, 4(1): 11–41.

Larson, J. and Gatto, L. (2005) Learning spaces travel: stepping in between the in/out of school binary, paper presented at the annual meeting of the American Educational Research Association, Montreal, April.

Larson, J. and Irvine, P.D. (1999) 'We call him Dr. King': reciprocal distancing in urban classrooms, *Language Arts*, 76(5): 393–400.

Larson, J. and Maier, M. (2000) Co-authoring classroom texts: shifting participant roles in writing activity, *Research in the Teaching of English*, 34: 468–98.

Larson, J. and Moll, L.C. (2000) Inspired by Vygotsky: ethnographic experiments in education, in C. Lee and P. Smagorinsky (eds), *Vygotskian Perspectives on Literacy Research: Constructing Meaning through Collaborative Inquiry*. pp. 256–68. New York: Cambridge University Press.

Larson, J. and Peterson, S.M. (2003) Talk and discourse in formal learning settings, in N. Hall, J. Larson and J. Marsh (eds), *Handbook of Early Childhood Literacy*. pp. 301–14. London: Sage/Paul Chapman Publishing.

Lave, J. and Wenger, E. (1991) *Situated Learning: Legitimate Peripheral Participation*. Cambridge: Cambridge University Press.

Leander, K. (2001) 'This is our freedom bus going home right now': producing and hybridizing space–time contexts in pedagogical discourse, *Journal of Literacy Research*, 33(4): 637–79.

Leander, K. and Sheehy, M. (eds) (2004) *Spatializing Literacy Research and Practice*. New York: Lang.

Leander, K.M. (2003) Writing travelers' tales on new literacyscapes, *Reading Research Quarterly*, 38(3): 392–97.

Leander, K.M. and McKim, K.K. (2003) Tracing the everyday 'sitings' of adolescents on the Internet: a strategic adaptation of ethnography across online and offline spaces, *Education, Communication, and Information*, 3(2): 211–40.

Lee, C. and Smagorinsky, P. (2000) *Vygotskian Perspectives on Literacy Research: Constructing Meaning through Collaborative Inquiry*. New York: Cambridge University Press.

Lee, C.D. (2001) Is October Brown Chinese? A cultural modeling activity system for underachieving students, *American Educational Research Journal*, 38(1): 97–142.

Lewis, C. (2001) *Literacy Practices as Social Acts: Power, Status and Cultural Norms in the Classroom*. Mahwah, NJ: Lawrence Erlbaum Associates.

Liem, Tik L. (1981) *Invitations to Science Inquiry*. 2nd edn. Chino Hills, CA: Science Inquiry Enterprises.

Lingard, B. (2005) Socially just pedagogies in changing times, paper presented to International Sociology of Education Conference, London, 3–5 January.

Livingstone, S. and Bovill, M. (1999) *Young People, New Media*. London: London School of Economics.

Loftus, G.R. and Loftus, E.E. (1983) *Mind at Play: The Psychology of Video Games*. New York: Basic Books.

Lortie, D. (1975) *Schoolteacher: A Sociological Study*. Chicago, IL: University of Chicago Press.

Luke, A. (1994) *The Social Construction of Literacy in the Primary School*. Melbourne: Macmillan.

Luke, A. (1995) Text and discourse in education: An introduction to critical discourse analysis, *Review of Research in Education*, 21: 3–48.

Luke, A. (2003) Literacy education for a new ethics of global community, *Language Arts*, 81(1): 20–2.

Luke, A. and Freebody, P. (1997a) Critical literacy and the question of normativity: an introduction, in S. Muspratt, A. Luke and P. Freebody (eds), *Constructing Critical Literacies: Teaching and Learning Textual Practice*. Sydney: Allen and Unwin.

Luke, A. and Freebody, P. (1997b) The social practices of reading, in S. Muspratt, A. Luke and P. Freebody (eds), *Constructing Critical Literacies: Teaching and Learning Textual Practice*. Sydney: Allen and Unwin.

Luke, A. and Freebody, P. (1999) A map of possible practices: further notes on the four resources model. At http//:www.readingonline.org/research/lukefreebody.html. Accessed November 2004.

Luke, A., Comber, B. and Grant, H. (2003) Critical literacies and cultural studies, in G. Bull and M. Anstey (eds), *The Literacy Lexicon*. 2nd edn. Melbourne: Prentice-Hall.

Marsh, J. (1999) Batman and Batwoman go to school: popular culture in the literacy curriculum, *International Journal of Early Years Education*, 7(2): 117–31.

Marsh, J. (2000a) Teletubby tales: popular culture in the early years language and literacy curriculum, *Contemporary Issues in Early Childhood*, 1(2): 119–36.

Marsh, J. (2000b) 'But I want to fly too!' Girls and superhero play in the infant classroom, *Gender and Education*, 12(2): 209-20.

Marsh, J. (2003a) One-way traffic? Connections between literacy practices at home and in the nursery, *British Educational Research Journal*, 29(3): 369–82.

Marsh, J. (2003b) Tightropes, tactics and taboos: An enquiry into the attitudes, beliefs and experiences of pre-service and newly qualified teachers with regard to the use of popular culture in the primary literacy curriculum, unpublished PhD thesis, Sheffield: University of Sheffield.

Marsh, J. (2004a) The primary canon: a critical review, *British Journal of Educational Studies*, 52(3): 249–62.

Marsh, J. (2004b) The techno-literacy practices of young children, *Journal of Early Childhood Research*, 2(1): 51–66.

Marsh, J. (ed.) (2005) *Popular Culture, New Media and Digital Literacy in Early Childhood*. London: RoutledgeFalmer.

Marsh, J. (forthcoming) Global, local/ public, private: young children's engagement in digital literacy practices in the home, in J. Rowsell and K. Pahl (eds), *Travel Notes from the New Literacy Studies: Case Studies in Practice*. Clevedon: Multilingual Matters.

Marsh, J. and Millard, E. (2000) *Literacy and Popular Culture: Using Children's Culture in the Classroom*. London: Paul Chapman Publishing/Sage.

Marsh, J. and Thompson, P. (2001) Parental involvement in literacy development: using media texts, *Journal of Research in Reading*, 24(3): 266–78.

McDiarmid, G. (1990) Tilting at webs: early field experiences as an occasion for breaking with experience, *Journal of Teacher Education*, 41(3): 12–20.

McFarlane, A., Sparrowhawk, A. and Heald, Y. (2002) *Report on the Educational Use of Games*. Cambridge: TEEM.

McIntyre, D.J., Byrd, D.M. and Foxx, S.M. (1996) Field and laboratory experiences, in J. Sikula, T.J. Buttery and E. Guyton. (eds), *Handbook of Research on Teacher Education*. New York: Simon and Schuster/Macmillan.

Meacham, S.J. (2003) Literacy and 'street credibility': plantations, prisons and African American literacy from Frederick Douglass to fifty cent, paper presented at ESRC Seminar Series Conference, University of Sheffield, 20 March.

Medwell, J., Wray, D., Poulson, L. and Fox, R. (1998) Effective teachers of literacy. EducationOn-line. At http:www.leeds.ac.uk/educol/. Accessed 26 January 2002.

Mehan, H. (1979) *Learning Lessons*. Cambridge, MA: Harvard University Press.

Merchant, G. (2001) Teenagers in cyberspace: language use and language change in Internet chatrooms, *Journal of Research in Reading*, 24(3): 293–306.

Merchant, G. (2004) Barbie meets Bob the Builder at the workstation: the word on screen/E-mergent literacies in the early years, in J. Marsh (ed.), *Popular Culture, Media and Digital Literacies in Early Childhood*. London: RoutledgeFalmer.

Merchant, G. (2005) Digikids: cool dudes and the new writing, *E-Learning*, 2(1): 50–60.

Mindscape (1995) Babyz software, Mindscape Entertainment.

Moll, L. (1990) *Vygotsky and Education*. New York: Cambridge University Press.

Moll, L. (2000) Inspired by Vygotsky: ethnographic experiments in education, in C. Lee and P. Smagorinsky (eds), *Vygotskian Perspectives on Literacy Research: Constructing Meaning through Collaborative Inquiry*. pp. 256–68. New York: Cambridge University Press.

Moll, L., Amanti, C., Neff, D. and Gonzalez, N. (1992) Funds of knowledge for teaching: using a qualitative approach to connect homes and classrooms, *Theory into Practice*, 31: 132–41.

Moss, G. (2000) Informal literacies and pedagogic discourse, *Linguistics and Education*, 11(1): 47–64.

Nespor, J. (1987) The role of beliefs in the practice of teaching, *Journal of Curriculum Studies*, (19)4: 317–28.

Nespor, J. (2000) School field trips and the curriculum of public spaces, *Journal of Curriculum Studies*, 32(1): 25–43.

New London Group (1996) A pedagogy of multiliteracies: designing social futures, *Harvard Educational Review*, 66(1): 60–92.

Nixon, H. and Comber, B. (2005) Behind the scenes: making movies in early years classrooms, in J. Marsh (ed.), *Popular Culture, Media and Digital Literacies in Early Childhood*. pp. 219–36. London: RoutledgeFalmer.

Nystrand, M. (1997) Dialogic instruction: when recitation becomes conversation, in M. Nystrand, with A. Gamoran, R. Kachur and C. Prendergrast (eds), *Opening Dialogue: Understanding the Dynamics of Language and Learning in the English Classroom.* pp. 1–29. New York: Teachers College Press.

O'Brien, J. and Comber, B. (2000) Negotiating critical literacies with young children, in C. Barratt-Pugh and M. Rohl (eds), *Literacy Learning in the Early Years.* Crows Nest, NSW: Allen and Unwin.

Ochs, E. (1988) *Culture and Language Development: Language Socialization and Language Acquisition in a Samoan Village.* Cambridge: Cambridge University Press.

Orellana, M.F. (1994) Appropriating the voice of the superheroes: three preschoolers' bilingual language uses in play, *Early Childhood Research Quarterly*, 9: 171–93.

Pahl, K. (2005) Narrative spaces and multiple identities: children's textual explorations of console games in home settings, in J. Marsh (ed.), *Popular Culture, New Media and Digital Literacy in Early Childhood.* London: RoutledgeFalmer.

Pajares, M. (1992) Teachers' beliefs and educational research: cleaning up a messy construct, *Review of Educational Research*, (62)3: 307–32.

Patrick-Diamond, C.T. (1991) *Teacher Education as Transformation.* Milton Keynes: Open University Press.

Piaget, J. (1926) *The Thought and Language of the Child.* New York: Harcourt Brace.

Pitchard, A. and Cartwright, V. (2004) Transforming what they read: helping eleven-year-olds engage with internet information, *Literacy*, 38(1): 26–31.

Pompe, C. (1996) 'But they're pink!' – 'Who cares!': popular culture in the primary years, in M. Hilton (ed.), *Potent Fictions: Children's Literacy and the Challenge of Popular Culture.* London: Routledge.

Prensky, M. (2001) *Digital Game-based Learning.* New York: McGraw-Hill.

Prensky, M. (2003) Beyond the exam, presentation at NESTA Futurelab Conference, Bristol, 19 November. At http://www.nestafuturelab.org/events/past/be_pres/m_prensky/mp01.htm.

Putney, L., Green, J., Dixon, D., Duran, R. and Yeager, B. (2000) Consequential progressions: exploring collective-individual development in a bilingual classroom, in C. Lee and P. Smagorinsky (eds), *Vygotskian Perspectives on Literacy Research: Constructing Meaning through Collaborative Inquiry.* pp. 86–126. New York: Cambridge University Press.

Reid, M., Burn, A. and Parker, D. (2002) *Evaluation Report of the BECTA Digital Video Pilot Project.* London: British Film Institute.

Rheingold, R. (2003) *Smartmobs: The Next Social Revolution*. New York: Perseus Publishing

Rideout, V.J., Vandewater, E.A. and Wartella, E.A. (2003) *Zero to Six: Electronic Media in the Lives of Infants, Toddlers and Preschoolers*. Washington, DC: Kaiser Foundation.

Robinson, M. (1997) *Children Reading Print and Television*. London: Falmer Press.

Rockhill, K. (1993) Dis/connecting literacy and sexuality: speaking the unspeakable in the classroom, in C. Lankshear and P. McLaren (eds), *Critical Literacy: Politics, Praxis, and the Postmodern*. Albany, NY: Suny Press.

Rogoff, B. (1990) *Apprenticeship in Thinking: Cognitive Development in Social Context*. New York: Oxford University Press.

Rogoff, B. (1992) Observing sociocultural activity on three planes: Participatory appropriation, guided participation, apprenticeship. Lecture presented at the Conference for Sociocultural Research, Madrid, Spain.

Rogoff, B. (1994) Developing understanding of the idea of communities of learners, *Mind, Culture, and Activity*, 1(4): 209–29.

Rogoff, B. (1995) Observing sociocultural activity on three planes: participatory appropriation, guided participation, and apprenticeship, in J.V. Wertsch, P. del Rio and A. Alvarez (eds), *Sociocultural Studies of Mind*. pp. 139–64. New York: Cambridge University Press.

Rogoff, B. (1996) Exploratorium Inquiry Forum , November (on-line). At http://www.exploratorium.edu/IFI/resources/inquirydesc.html#hubertd. Accessed 5 November 2002.

Rogoff, B. (2003) *The Cultural Nature of Human Development*. Oxford: Oxford University Press.

Rogoff, B., Goodman-Turkanis, C. and Bartlett, L. (2001) *Learning Together: Children and Adults in a School Community*. Oxford: Oxford University Press.

Rose, M. (1995) *Possible Lives*. Boston, MA: Houghton-Mifflin.

Ross, V. (2003) Walking around the curriculum tree: an analysis of a third/fourth grade mathematics lesson, *Journal of Curriculum Studies*, 35(5): 567–84.

Saracho, O. and Spodek, B. (1993) Introduction: language and literacy in early childhood education, in B. Spodek and O. Saracho (eds), *Language and Literacy in Early Childhood Education*. pp. vii–xiii. New York: Teachers College Press.

Schrage, M. (1997) Technology, silver bullets, and big lies, *Educom Review*, 33(1): 32–7.

Schrage, M. (1998) Technology, silver bullets and big lies: musings on the information age with author Michael Schrage. At www.educause.edu/pub/er/review/reviewArticles/33132.html. Accessed 26 January 2000.

Schrage, M. (2000) The relationship revolution. At http://www.seedwiki.com/page.cfm?doc=The%20Relationship%20Revolutionandwikiid=6717. Accessed 20 January 2004.

Scribner, S. (1990) Reflections on a model, *Quarterly Newsletter of the Laboratory of Comparative Human Cognition*, 12: 90–4.

Scribner, S. and Cole, M. (1981) *The Psychology of Literacy*. Cambridge, MA: Harvard University Press.

Shannon, P. (1992) Commercial reading materials, a technological ideology, and the deskilling of teachers, in P. Shannon (ed.), *Becoming Political: Readings and Writings in the Politics of Literacy Education*. Portsmouth, NH: Heinemann.

Sheehy, M. and Leander, K.M. (2004) Introduction, in K. Leander and M. Sheehy (eds), *Spatializing Literacy Research and Practice*. pp. 1–13. New York: Lang.

Shor, I. (1992) *Empowering Education: Critical Teaching for Social Change*. Chicago, IL: University of Chicago Press.

Shor, I. (1996) *When Students Have Power: Negotiating Authority in a Critical Pedagogy*. Chicago, IL: University of Chicago Press.

Shor, I. and Freire, P. (1987a) *A Pedagogy for Liberation: Dialogues on Transforming Education*. South Hadley, MA: Bergin and Garvey.

Shor, I. and Freire, P. (1987b) What is the 'dialogical method' of teaching? *Journal of Education*, 169(3): 11–31.

Short, K.G., Harste, J.C. and Burke, C. (1996) *Creating Classrooms for Authors and Inquirers*. 2nd edn. Portsmouth, NH: Heinemann.

Shulman, L. (1987) Knowledge and teaching: foundations of the new reform, *Harvard Educational Review*, (57)1: 1–22.

Shulman, L. and Shulman, J. (2004) How and what teachers learn: a shifting perspective, *Journal of Curriculum Studies*, 36(2): 257–71.

Smith, D. and Larson, J. (2004) *Unpacking Effective Practice*. Rochester, NY: University of Rochester.

Street, B. (1984) *Literacy in Theory and Practice*. New York: Cambridge University Press.

Street, B. (ed.) (1993) *Cross-cultural Approaches to Literacy*. London: Cambridge University Press.

Street, B. (1995) *Social Literacies: Critical Approaches to Literacy in Development, Ethnography, and Education*. London: Longman.

Street, B (1997) The implications of the new literacy studies for literacy education, *English in Education*, 31(3): 45–59.

Street, B. (1999) New literacies in theory and practice: what are the implications for language in education? *Linguistics and Education*, 10(1), 1–24.

Street, B. (2003) What's 'new' in new literacy studies? Critical approaches to literacy in theory and practice, *Current Issues in Comparative Education*, 5(2): 1–14.

Street, B. (2004) Academic literacies and the 'new orders': implications for research and practice in student writing in higher education, *Learning and Teaching in the Social Sciences*, 1(1): 9–32.

Street, B. (ed.) (2005) *Literacies across Educational Contexts: Mediating Teaching and Learning*. Philadelphia, PA: Caslon Press.

Street, B. (forthcoming) Reading, multiple literacies and multiliteracy, *Encyclopedia of Language and Linguistics: Language Learning and Teaching*.

Street, B., Baker, D. and Tomalin, A. (forthcoming) *Navigating Numeracies: Home/School Numeracy Practice*. Vol. 4 of series on Leverhulme Numeracy Research. Dordrecht: Kluwer.

Sulzby, E. (1989) Assessment of writing and of children's language while writing, in L. Morrow and J. Smith (eds), *The Role of Assessment and Measurement In Early Literacy Instruction*. pp. 83–109. Englewood Cliffs, NJ: Prentice Hall.

Thomas, A. (2004) Children online: learning in a virtual community of practice, *E learning*, 1 (4). At http://www.wwwords.co.uk/elea/ (forthcoming).

Thomas, A. (2005) *E-selves|e-literacies|e-worlds: Children's Identities and Literacies in Virtual Communities*. New York: Lang.

Tunbridge, N. (1995) The cyberspace cowboy, *Australian Personal Computer*, December: 2–4.

Turbill, J. (2001) A researcher goes to school: using new technology in the kindergarten literacy curriculum, *Journal of Early Childhood Literacy*, (1)3: 255–79.

Vasquez, V. (2001) Constructing a critical curriculum with young children, in B. Comber and A. Simpson (eds), *Negotiating Critical Literacies in Classrooms*. Mahwah, NJ, and London: Lawrence Erlbaum Associates.

Vasquez, V. (2004a) *Negotiating Critical Literacies with Young Children*. Mahwah, NJ, and London: Lawrence Erlbaum Associates.

Vasquez, V. (2004b) Resistance, power-tricky, and colorless energy: what engagement with everyday popular culture texts can teach us about learning, and literacy, in J. Marsh (ed.), *Popular Culture, New Media and Digital Literacy in Early Childhood*. London: RoutledgeFalmer.

Vicars, M. (forthcoming) I have a feeling we're not in Kansas any more: a British gay educator's reconstructed life-history account of school, *Sex Education*, 5(4).

Vygotsky, L.S. (1962) *Thought and Language*. Cambridge, MA: MIT Press.

Vygotsky, L.S. (1978) *Mind in Society: The Development of Higher Psychological Processes*. Cambridge, MA: Harvard University Press.

Webb, J., Schirato, T. and Danaher, G. (2002) *Understanding Bourdieu*. London: Sage.

Wells, G. (1999) *Dialogic Inquiry: Toward a Sociocultural Practice and Theory of Education*. New York: Cambridge University Press.

Wells, G. (2000) Dialogic inquiry in education: building on the legacy of Vygotsky, in C. Lee and P. Smagorinsky (eds), *Vygotskian Perspectives on Literacy Research*. Cambridge: Cambridge University Press.

Wertsch, J.V. (1991) *Voices of The Mind: A Sociocultural Approach to Mediated Action*. Cambridge: Cambridge University Press.

Wertsch, J.V., del Rio, P. and Alvarez, A. (1995) *Sociocultural Studies of Mind*. New York: Cambridge University Press.

Whitebread, D. (1997) Developing children's problem-solving: the educational uses of adventure games, in A McFarlane (ed.), *Information Technology and Authentic Learning*. London: Routledge.

Woods, A.F. (2004) The contexts and purposes of school literacy pedagogy: 'failing' in the early years, unpublished PhD dissertation, University of Queensland, Australia.

Author Index

Added to the page number 'n' denotes a footnote.

A

Alvermann, D. 44, 148, 149
Anderson, G. 45
Atwell, N. 21, 116

B

Bakhtin, M.M. 12, 104
Ball, A. 28, 103
Bartlett, L. 101, 102, 106, 109, 118, 119, 123, 137
Barton, D. 1, 10, 12, 19, 20, 22, 23, 69, 146, 155
Belton, T. 149
Berger, A.A. 78
Berger, P. 10
Bernstein, B. 6, 7, 8, 17, 81, 82, 154
Bigum, C. 72, 91, 92, 94, 97, 98
Bloome, D. 13, 25
Bourdieu, P. 6, 152
Bovill, M. 70, 73
Brady, J. 44
Bredekamp, S. 104
Britzman, D.P. 151, 152
Brooker, L. 153
Bruner, J. 105

Buckingham, D. 69
Burke, C. 28
Burn, A. 69, 76
Burnett, C. 74, 79, 83, 89
Byrd, D.M. 150

C

Calkins, L. 21
Carrington, V. 5, 68, 73
Carter, K. 150
Cartwright, V. 83
Cazden, C. 12
Certeau, M. de 23, 28, 72
Civil, M. 151
Clandinin, D.J. 151
Cocking, R.R. 78
Cole, M. 18, 19, 28, 100, 101, 102, 103, 109, 110, 118
Comber, B. 45, 46, 47, 50, 61, 62, 65, 66, 68, 91, 127, 133, 134, 135, 139, 149, 155
Cope, B. 23, 44, 68-9, 139

D

Daiute, C. 106
Danaher, G. 152
Davidson, C.R. 133
Davies, J. 133, 155

Subject Index

Added to the page number 'f' denotes a figure and 't' denotes a table.

A
access issues in critical literacy 44
accountability 21, 142
acquisition theories of learning 9
advertising 64
'affinity spaces' 133
African-Americans, literacy practices 44
apprenticeship 108
'at risk' children 5
attitudes, effect on teachers' practice 151
Australia, use of critical literacy 42, 66
authentic activities 28, 31–2
autonomous models of literacy 11, 20, 22

B
'banking' models of education 41
beliefs, effect on teachers' practice 151
Bernstein's conceptual tools 6–8
'blogging' 137
'blue sky thinking' 74
bricolage, concept of 72

C
changing participation, learning as 2, 9–10, 100, 103, 105–6, 127
choice, offering 29

CLA (critical language awareness) 43–4
classification
  concept 6
  see also strong classification; weak classification
classroom discourse 12–13, 14t
classrooms
  contribution of researching techno-literacy practices 94–5
  and critical literacy
    contribution to practice 63
    implementation of a framework 65–6
    implications 42–6
  implications of new technologies 71–6
  literacy events and practices in 129f
  and NLS
    connecting propositions to practices 24–5
    contribution to practice 37
    implications 21–5
  and sociocultural-historical theory
    contribution to practice 123
    implementation of a framework 123–4
    implications 101, 105–9
co-construction
  of knowledge 28, 29, 73, 104
  of literacy learning 106
cognitive development, stages 103–4

MORE LITERACY TITLES

from SAGE Publications, Paul Chapman Publishing and Lucky Duck

Learning Through Talk in the Early Years

Practical Activities for the Classroom

Elizabeth Sharp *Literacy Consultant, Milton Keynes*

Lots of ideas and suggestions for activities using and encouraging talk in the classroom make this book a lively, practical guide to encouraging young children to develop their verbal reasoning skills and to communicate more effectively.

There is advice on how to tie in these activities with the various curriculum subjects and the following are covered: setting up a talk corner, using story bags and story boxes, and using Circle Time and playing games to encourage talk.

In each activity there are directions for helping children with Special Educational Needs, working with teaching assistants and other adults in the classroom, planning and assessing work and finding suitable resources.

A selection of photocopiable material is included and all the suggestions and ideas in the book have been tried and tested by the author in her own classroom. The focus of this book is on young children aged five to eight years, but the activities can be adapted to suit those younger and older.

Contents
How to use this Book \ Songs, Poetry and Rhymes \ Home Corners and Talk Areas \ Drama, Role Play and Mime \ Story Boxes, Story Bags and Story-Telling \ Debating and Questioning \ Pictures and Picture Books \ Circle Time and Talk Games

Paul Chapman Publishing
August 2005 • 128 pages
Cloth (1-4129-0310-6) / Paper (1-4129-0311-4)

Write Dance in the Nursery

A Pre-Writing Programme for Children 3 to 5

Ragnhild Oussoren

Write Dance is an innovative and exciting programme, widely used across Europe as a way of introducing handwriting using music, movement and exercise. It has been found especially helpful for children with special educational needs, from learning difficulties to dyspraxia.

In **Write Dance in the Nursery**, early years practitioners are provided with a new package of songs, stories and role play ideas designed especially for their settings. Supporting child-initiated play within the foundation curriculum and the 'Birth to Three Matters' framework, these provide an introduction to the nine themes in Write Dance approach at an appropriate developmental level.

The children are encouraged to experience all the Write Dance movements, with the aim of making them feel happy and comfortable with their bodies.

Contents
What is Write Dance? \ Toddler-Write Dance \ Movements in Your Space \ Movements on a Writing Surface \ Both Hands \ Consolidating \ Experiencing and Emotions \ Repetition and Routine \ Development \ Scrambling Area \ Materials for the Writing Surface \ Writing Materials \ Materials for Theme Play \ The Role of the Teacher \ A Ten-Steps Working Method for Toddler-Write Dance \ Stories \ Movements \ Theme Play \ Scrambling

Lucky Duck Books
September 2005 • 91 pages
Cloth (1-4129-2172-4) / Paper (1-4129-1904-5)

Early Literacy Work with Families

Policy, Practice and Research

Cathy Nutbrown, Peter Hannon and **Anne Morgan** *all at University of Sheffield*

'Essential reading for anyone working alongside families to promote children's early development' - *Professor Nigel Hall, Institute of Education, Manchester Metropolitan University*

Anyone involved in the field of early childhood literacy should be familiar with the work of the Raising Early Achievement in Literacy (REAL) Project. Here, leading members of the project team, Cathy Nutbrown, Peter Hannon and Anne Morgan discuss the research.

The book includes: a description of the family literacy programme; useful activities for family literacy work!; guidelines for interviewing parents and children; suggestions for how to evaluate family literacy work; and ideas for practical sessions for professional development of family literacy workers.

Contents
EARLY CHILDHOOD EDUCATION AND FAMILY LITERACY: POLICY CONTEXTS \ Early Childhood Education: Policy Contexts \ Family Literacy: Policy Contexts \ DEVELOPING A FAMILY LITERACY PROJECT: RESEARCH, EVALUATION AND EXPERIENCE \ Developing Family Literacy Work in ECE Settings \ Professional Development for Family Literacy Workers \ The Importance of Planning and Evaluation \ PERSPECTIVES AND EVALUATION \ Practitioners' Perspectives on Family Literacy \ Parents' Perspectives on Family Literacy \ Children's Perspectives of Family Literacy \ Can Early Literacy Work With Children Make A Difference To Their Early Literacy Development? \ THE FUTURE FOR EARLY CHILDHOOD EDUCATION AND FAMILY LITERACY \ Practices and Processes in Early Literacy Work with Parents

September 2005 • 216 pages
Cloth (1-4129-0374-2) / Paper (1-4129-0375-0)

Read sample chapters and order online at **www.PaulChapmanPublishing.co.uk**

Paul Chapman Publishing
A SAGE Publications Company

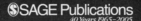
SAGE Publications
40 Years 1965-2005

Lucky Duck Publishing